MW01199382

Angela of Foligno's *Memorial*

Library of Medieval Women ISSN 1369-9652

Series Editor: Jane Chance

Already published

Christine de Pizan's Letter of Othea to Hector, *Jane Chance*, 1990

The Writings of Margaret of Oingt, Medieval Prioress and Mystic, *Renate Blumenfeld-Kosinski*, 1990

Saint Bride and her Book: Birgitta of Sweden's Revelations, *Julia Bolton Holloway*, 1992

The Memoirs of Helene Kottanner (1439–1440), *Maya Bijvoet Williamson*, 1998

The Writings of Teresa de Cartagena, *Dayle Seidenspinner-Núñez*, 1998

Julian of Norwich: *Revelations of Divine Love* and *The Motherhood of God*, *Frances Beer*, 1998

Hrotsvit of Gandersheim: A Florilegium of her Works, *Katharina M. Wilson*, 1998

Hildegard of Bingen: On Natural Philosophy and Medicine: Selections from *Cause et cure, Margret Berger*, 1999

Women Saints' Lives in Old English Prose, *Leslie A. Donovan*, 1999

Angela of Foligno's *Memorial*

Translated from Latin
with Introduction, Notes and Interpretive Essay

Cristina Mazzoni
University of Vermont

Translation by
John Cirignano
University of Vermont

D.S. BREWER

First published 1999
D. S. Brewer, Cambridge

Transferred to digital printing

ISBN 978-0-85991-562-5

D. S. Brewer is an imprint of Boydell & Brewer Ltd
PO Box 9, Woodbridge, Suffolk IP12 3DF, UK
and of Boydell & Brewer Inc.
668 Mt Hope Avenue, Rochester, NY 14620, USA
website: www.boydellandbrewer.com

A CiP catalogue record for this book is available
from the British Library

This publication is printed on acid-free paper

Contents

Corrigenda

Introduction, section 2

[pp. 3–4]

For the overview of the role of women in medieval Italy, I am indebted to Daniel Bornstein, "Women and Religion in Late Medieval Italy: History and Historiography," in *Women and Religion in Medieval and Renaissance Italy*, eds. Daniel Bornstein and Robert Rusconi, trans. Margery J. Schneider (Chicago: University of Chicago Press, 1996), 1–27.

[p. 5]

An in-depth discussion of saintly women's rupture of the ordinary frameworks for the life of medieval women may be found in Anna Benvenuti Papi, "Mendicant Friars and Female Pinzochere in Tuscany: From Social Marginality to Models of Sanctity," in Bornstein and Rusconi, 84–103.

In memory of
Ruth V.K. Pakaluk (1957–1998)

filia Dei legitima

Preface and Acknowledgments

The past decade or so has witnessed a striking and prolific renewal of critical interest in the writings of women mystics. Unlike many earlier analyses, recent criticism of mysticism often develops interpretations which are neither hagiographical nor simplistically reductive. These readings are frequently informed by psychoanalysis and/or feminism, but although they do not take the orthodox position of the Church, they are nevertheless sympathetic to the mystic and her text and do not merely discard her voice as impossibly distant or, even worse, hopelessly pathological. I mention many of these articles and books in the annotated bibliography found at the end of this volume. Furthermore, thanks in part to Paul Lachance's excellent translation of Angela's complete works (published in the Classics of Spirituality Series in 1993), English-speaking critics have had access to Angela's writings and have been able to incorporate them in their readings.

The translation presented here offers a selection from the *Memorial*, the first part of Angela's *Book*. The text on which John Cirignano's translation is based is the 1985 edition by Ludger Thier and Abele Calufetti – not a perfect edition, but the best one currently available. The translation remains very close to Angela's text, and every attempt was made to preserve Angela's colloquial tone. The entire *Memorial* unfortunately could not be included for reasons of space, and Angela's text is so rich that each cut was a painful one. I included as much as possible about the role of the body and its interaction with the soul in Angela's mystical experience, since the fascination exerted by the history of the body is one of the reasons why the works of the mystics have recently claimed so much critical attention. In making editorial choices, I also focused on the way in which the *Memorial* came about, namely through the collaboration between Angela and her scribe, and I preserved most of the text that alludes to or explicitly deals with such collaboration. The link between power and writing, essential to this collaboration, is also central to the contemporary study of mystical texts, and it should be of great interest for anyone who studies the history of women as well as literary theory. For every section of the *Memorial* that was excluded, I have provided a brief summary. These summaries are italicized throughout the text and indicate where the cuts have taken place.

The footnotes to the selections of the *Memorial* are meant to give historical, cultural, and textual guidance throughout a text that is often challenging in many ways. The interpretive essay that follows the text compares the issues addressed by Angela of Foligno in the *Memorial* to those discussed in the writings of contemporary feminist theologians. This comparison should allow today's reader to understand both the profound differences and the striking continuities between a medieval woman mystic and many contemporary Christian women.

The interpretive essay is followed by a selection of brief texts of women mystics who were Angela's contemporaries and with whom Angela had much in common. Each of these figures is introduced by a biographical and critical profile. John Cirignano's translation of their works is based on Latin texts found in Giovanni Pozzi's and Claudio Leonardi's critical anthology *Scrittrici mistiche italiane*. Umiltà of Faenza, Margherita of Cortona, Vanna of Orvieto, and Chiara of Montefalco provide us with a context of little-heard female voices which underline both Angela's extraordinariness and her continuity with an important female culture.

In the many years that I have been involved with the study of women mystics, I have received much help and encouragement from many different people in many different ways. To my husband John Cirignano, first of all, I owe a marvelous translation, insightful and constructive comments, and plenty of comic relief on the margins. This was truly a collaborative effort, not only from an intellectual viewpoint, but especially as each of us took care of our three small children while the other was absorbed by the relatively easier task of research and writing. Paul, Gemma, and Sophia have in turn filled our life with joy and blessings – ineffable like Angela's.

There are two other people without whom this book would not have been written. Although I have never physically met either of them, we have been regular correspondents during the years of my involvement with Angela: Jane Chance, who has been a wonderfully supportive editor, as well as a prompt and constructive reader; and Paul Lachance, whose translation has been an inspiration, and whose extensive scholarship on Angela continues to be an indispensable reference that is never allowed to wander too far away from my reach.

Finally, Valerie Lagorio's seminar on the mystics at the University of Iowa motivated me to read and write about the mystics themselves and not just about their detractors. Her advice to 'fish or cut bait' to both me and my husband has proved to yield fruitful results in more ways than one.

Introduction

1. Angela of Foligno's life

Angela of Foligno is little-known today, yet she is one of the greatest Italian mystics of the Christian tradition. She was beatified by the Catholic Church on July 11, 1701, several hundred years after her death, and although many admirers refer to her as Saint Angela, she was never canonized. The scarcity of information about this medieval Italian woman's life is matched only by the abundance of details she has left behind concerning her spiritual journey and her numerous encounters with God. In fact, if we can reconstruct some of Angela's experiences in this world, this is primarily thanks to some occasional and often elliptical references that are scattered throughout her religious writings. The only clear chronological information, for example, is that Angela fell into a deep spiritual crisis shortly before the election of Pope Celestine V, therefore between April 1292 and July 1294. The other dates have been deduced by scholars on the basis of the time lapsed between the various phases of Angela's spiritual journey.

Angela's birth is conjectured to have taken place in Foligno, an Umbrian center of Franciscan spirituality just a few miles from Assisi, in 1248. For many years, Angela led what she later condemned as a sinful because sensuous and superficial existence, but in spite of numerous speculations we in fact know nothing with certainty concerning the actual nature of her sins. Though not formally educated, Angela most likely knew how to read (and, maybe, even write) and, like other holy women of her time, had a learned culture of her own: her text contains echoes of philosophical and religious texts as well as scriptural reminiscences. The latter are thematic as well as linguistic, yet it is worth noting that Angela's *Memorial* is uncharacteristically poor in scriptural citations. Angela – or Lella, the diminutive through which, as a sign of humility, she also came to be known – married sometime after the age of twenty, perhaps around 1270, and had children. But after her conversion around 1285, and this is one of the best-known and even somewhat scandalous aspects of Angela's story, she prayed for the death of her entire family. When her mother, husband, and children all died within a brief span of time, Angela thanked God because she was freed of those family ties that precluded a primary commitment to the religious life. Family was for Angela an obstacle for both practical and spiritual reasons. The topos of the family as a barrier to holiness has in fact a long tradition in Christian thought: Angela follows Christ's dictum in Luke 14:26, whereby rejection of one's family is a precondition to true discipleship. Marriage was in fact perceived as an impediment by many medieval holy women, who found in the religious life that freedom and autonomy unavailable to them in the secular world.

If the consolation Angela found in the death of her family has to be tempered by her later admission of grief over the deaths of her mother and children (though, interestingly enough, not of her husband), still the exultation she declared concerning her ability to finally follow and imitate the crucified Christ – thanks to the demise of those people whom in this world she most dearly loved – does, and indeed must continue to carry its shocking impact. Only without them could she espouse celibacy. Only without them could she wholly renounce the ways of the world and, naked like Saint Francis and Christ himself, follow the way of the cross (the theme of spiritual nudity, of following naked the crucified Christ, was common during the medieval period and was developed especially by Saint Bonaventure).

In addition to quite literally shedding off all her clothes in front of the cross as a gesture of self-giving – a gesture that finds echoes in past theology and hagiography, but which Angela carries out with unprecedented audacity – Angela stripped herself of all her worldly riches, which she distributed to the poor, and entered the Third Order of Saint Francis between 1290 and 1291 (the Third Order had just become a distinct organization in 1289 with the bull *Supra Montem* of Pope Nicholas IV, a Franciscan). Poverty was for Angela a worldly reflection of our human condition with respect to God, a condition fully assumed by Christ himself through the Incarnation. In 1291 Angela made a pilgrimage to Assisi with a group that included her constant companion, referred to as M. and commonly named, though without any documentary evidence, Masazuola. We know very little about Masazuola in spite of her frequent appearances in Angela's *Liber*: she was most likely Angela's servant as well as her confidante. In the Basilica of Saint Francis in Assisi Angela had a spectacular mystical crisis, a direct and internal encounter with God. That this crisis should have happened in Assisi is no coincidence, for the spirituality of the Poverello, i.e. Saint Francis, is central to Angela's own. As the feeling of God's proximity dissipated, it led Angela to repeatedly cry out the same phrase over and over again:

"Love unknown, why, why, why?!" (43).[1] Angela's cry eventually turned into an inarticulate sound as she lay thrashing on the pavement of the Basilica. After this scandalous episode, her embarrassed relative, confessor, and, later, scribe, who was at that time a member of the Sacro Convento in Assisi, forbade her from ever returning to Assisi. About this Franciscan Friar Minor, so important for Angela's story and central to the composition of her *Memorial*, we know next to nothing: he is usually identified by biographical tradition as Brother Arnaldo, or Brother A., but even this is without any reliable evidence.

When, shortly thereafter, he returned to Foligno as a member of the friary affiliated with the Church of Saint Francis, the scribe encouraged Angela to recount to him her experiences so that he could assess whether it was God or the devil that was at work within her soul and body. Between 1292 and 1296 Angela dictated the *Memorial* to her scribe, most of the time while sitting in the Church of Saint Francis in Foligno. The text, an autobiography-diary, was approved by Cardinal Giacomo Colonna probably in 1296, and certainly before May 1297. I return to the composition, structure, and content of the *Memorial* in the third section of this Introduction.

It was probably in 1298 that Angela received the visit of Ubertino of Casale, controversial leader of the Spiritual Franciscans. Ubertino had been attracted to Angela's doctrine during his stay in Paris, and he attributed his conversion to radical asceticism to Angela in his treatise *Arbor vitae crucifixae Jesu*. Angela quickly became a known and venerable figure who attracted a sizable following of men and women, clergy and laity, for whom she had the role of spiritual mother. Thus tradition has bestowed upon Angela the impressive title of *Magistra theologorum*, Master of theologians. In spite of her harshly penitential life and intense work at the service of the sick and the outcast, feeding and caring for them, Angela lived to be over sixty, an unusually long life for a holy woman of her time. We know nothing of the last few years of Angela's life. She died in Foligno in the year 1309, on January 4, the day when her feast is now celebrated. Her remains, appropriately buried in the Church of Saint Francis in Foligno, started attracting many devout men and women shortly after her death.

2. Angela's cultural-historical context: medieval mysticism
Angela of Foligno is often said to have parallels only abroad, in Northern Europe, with great mystics such as Mechtild of Magdeburg and Mechtild of Hackeborn, Hadewijch, Beatrice of Nazareth,

---

[1] All page numbers refer to John Cirignano's translation in this book.

Gertrud of Helfta and Marguerite Porete. Yet despite her unquestionably exceptional stature, Angela of Foligno is an eloquent example of the often paradoxical status of women in medieval Italy. Her public role of religious prominence contradicts the institutional and ideological inferiority to which women, including Angela, were at that time condemned: they were barred from political and ecclesiastical office, subjected to the authority of their male relatives, excluded from institutions of higher education, and, most pervasively, associated in theology, philosophy, and popular culture with the lower fleshly substratum of humanity. As we have seen, Angela herself, despite her charisma and visions, had to wait and even pray for the death of her family before she could pursue her religious vocation. And it was the sacred charisma brought about by an exceptional visionary experience that bestowed on Angela of Foligno, and on many other women who were more or less her contemporaries, the ability to be heard, believed, and even followed. Angela states clearly in her *Memorial*: "because my soul is often elevated into divine secrets and sees God's secrets, I understand how Holy Scripture came to be, how it is both easy and difficult, how it seems to contradict itself, how those who do not observe Scripture's teachings are damned and how it is fulfilled in them, and how others who do observe its teachings are saved; I see all this from above" (75).

Men were indeed less likely than women to have visions, and if they did, they were still unlikely to put them at the center of their spiritual paths; but men were also less in need of special validation, for unlike women they had access to formal education and ecclesiastical positions. On the other hand, this access was made unnecessary, in the case of many medieval holy women, by direct contact with the divinity as manifested in visionary experience. It is around Angela's time that women acquire and vigorously exercise an unprecedented role in the history of Christianity, whether in religious communities, in solitary penitence, in heremitic contemplation, or in practical assistance to the needy. The percentage of women proclaimed saints around this time rises rapidly, so that historians of spirituality have talked about a veritable "feminization" of recognized sanctity in the Roman Catholic Church starting in the thirteenth century.[2] Franciscanism played an important role in this tendency, and

---

[2] André Vauchez, "L'idéal de sainteté dans le mouvement féminin franciscain aux XIIIe et XIVe siècles," in *Movimento religioso femminile e francescanesimo nel secolo XIII*. Atti del VII Convegno Internazionale, Assisi, 11–13 ottobre 1979 (Assisi: Società Editrice di Studi Francescani, 1980): 315–337, 319.

Angela's home region, Umbria – Saint Francis's own region as well – was a privileged area for women's spiritual growth.

Rather than conform to the older, virginal model of female sanctity, Angela had been married and borne children, and was later widowed. The exceptional spiritual experiences of Angela and her contemporaries (such as, for example, Umiltà of Faenza, Margherita of Cortona, Vanna of Orvieto, and Chiara of Montefalco, to whose texts I briefly return later in this book)[3] can be related to their socially marginal position with respect to family and convent, i.e., the ordinary frameworks for the life of medieval women. It was perhaps this very marginality that allowed a mobility otherwise impossible to the majority of medieval women, who were firmly planted in ideologically and structurally stable settings. This type of lay, as opposed to monastic, sanctity was made possible in part by the experience of Saint Francis of Assisi, which is why, at least since the end of the twelfth century, women saints may be seen as important depositories of Francis's heritage, whether or not they were officially associated with the Franciscan Order. It cannot be a coincidence that of all the women that were the object of an official canonization process between 1198 and 1431 (dates which do not even include important figures such as Angela of Foligno, Umiliana de' Cerchi, and Margherita of Cortona), five, namely half of them, were connected with the Franciscan movement.[4] Like Francis's, their experience of God is direct and unmediated, lay rather than clerical, though this ascent to the divine is complemented by a descent into humanity, through an active involvement in matters of this world – above all, service of the poor and the sick as well as spiritual and ecclesiastical reform. Furthermore, like Saint Francis's experience, Angela's own centered on a love of poverty and solitary prayer, adoration of and identification with the Passion and the Eucharist, devotion to the Virgin Mary and the angels, and joyful encounters with suffering – especially the suffering of the lepers.

Mysticism is "the only place in the history of the West in which woman speaks and acts so publicly," feminist theorist Luce Irigaray has famously and hyperbolically pronounced in her influential treatise, *Speculum of the Other Woman*.[5] If limited to the medieval

---

3 An introduction to these authors and selections from their texts can be found at the end of this book.

4 Vauchez, 317.

5 Luce Irigaray, *Speculum of the Other Woman*, trans. Gillian Gill (Ithaca: Cornell University Press, 1985), 191.

period, this statement is an accurate one. Mystical experience is directly connected to power, for acknowledged access to God's will puts the mystic in the position of challenging every other form of authority. And during the Middle Ages, mystical experience and hence an authority of divine origins was at the basis of women's public reputation and empowerment as spiritual leaders (as prophets, visionaries, healers) more often than it was for men. Hence the discussion mysticism has provoked, especially in recent years and in feminist circles, about the close links between power and gender. Many reasons, cultural, historical, and psychological, have been advanced for this connection between women and mysticism, and indeed no single explanation can be considered the privileged one. Rather, a complex set of circumstances has gendered the flowering of medieval European mysticism as peculiarly female.

Some explanations have been adduced for quite some time. First of all, women were excluded from the public sacramental life of the Church: the only approved form of religious life was for them contemplative and enclosed (an isolation not unrelated to the association between woman and the evils of the flesh) and some aspects of convent existence fostered the development of mystical life: the opportunity to read and write, access to privacy and to a library, the availability of positions of leadership and teaching. Those holy women who remained outside the convent, be they part of a Third Order or not, shared with their cloistered sisters certain practical features of lifestyle, such as celibacy (necessary for privacy, as we have seen in the case of Angela – who must wait for her family to die before she can devote herself to Christ), spiritual practices (including a kind of visual meditation that often led to visions), and opportunities for leadership.

From a quantitative viewpoint, one must mention what is commonly known to historians as the "woman question." For the first time women outnumbered men in medieval Europe, so that not all women could possibly fulfill society's expectations and get married. Many, instead, came together as penitents to form non-cloistered and, at least at the beginning, relatively unstructured religious communities, lacking permanent vows, called Beguines in Northern Europe and Tertiaries – Franciscan or Dominican – in Southern Europe. Beguines, however, lived communally, in a semi-monastic lifestyle, while Tertiaries preferred to remain in their own homes. The Third Order was neither strictly religious nor altogether secular, and as such it was the preferred choice of a number of mystics: for example, we can think, in addition to Blessed Angela of Foligno, of her contemporary Saint Margaret of Cortona. Tertiaries had to attend Mass and fast regularly, go to confession and receive Communion three times a year, recite certain prayers daily, wear simple grey or black clothes, and perform service to the poor and sick. Furthermore, widows and the unmarried were to abstain from any sexual activity. Both Beguines and Tertiaries, in part because of their radical interpretation of the Gospel, were often mixed up with heretical movements. Hence Angela's frequent protestations in her writings against the Sect of the Spirit of Freedom, a heretical group with whose practices and beliefs her own spiritual life, as I explain below, actually had several elements in common.

The perspective of cultural studies has more recently argued that women's oppressed social situation made them more likely to be drawn to radical forms of religious experience such as mysticism. In particular, a bodily expression of spirituality was in a sense to be expected given women's different relation to and closer association with their body and to the very concept of embodiment – including, then, not only the negative, evil flesh, but also the redemptive body of Christ. For in the doctrine of the Incarnation, Christ's physical humanity, his flesh, was gendered as female: by dying, Christ's flesh metaphorically gave birth to new life, it provided spiritual food in the form of the Eucharist, and it was thought to come entirely from his mother – the only human parent of Jesus as well as, in the Aristotelian physiology still prevalent in the Middle Ages, the only source of any fetus's flesh. The Incarnation informed the spirituality of medieval holy women as well as our own modern notion of what constitutes mysticism. The body was for medieval holy women, in the eloquent words of André Vauchez, "a privileged instrument of communication."[6] Through exceptional phenomena such as stigmata, levitation, ecstasy, and visions, the body, and particularly the female body, could spell out what was otherwise ineffable and could not be grasped by words. The *Brautmystik*, or bridal mysticism, problematically gendered as female and also known as affective mysticism, celebrates the love affair of the soul with God, as well as of the woman mystic with Christ, and abounds in erotic imagery. This sort of mysticism flourished among the Beguines of the Low Countries and, although present and important in Angela's *Memorial*, it is certainly not its essence. Women's mysticism is usually characterized by harsh asceticism, which in turn led to a variety of paranormal bodily phenomena, such as levitation and bleeding stigmata.

6 Vauchez, 337. My translation.

But what is most important for any reading of female-authored mystical texts are those bodily metaphors and images contained therein, for these, more than the hagiographer's descriptions, are crucial vectors of women's visionary experiences. These textual practices help us understand not only women's peculiar compatibility with the mystical life but also its tolerance by an institutional Church whose own authority was often undermined by some of the mystics' more subversive claims. The most dangerous of these was the apparent denial of the need for any intermediary (such as the Church, its priests, and its sacraments) between the mystic and God – one of the tenets of the heretical sect of the Spirit of Freedom. Angela herself at certain points in the *Memorial* seems to bypass the need for clerical and/or ecclesiastical intercession, such as when a leper's scab tastes to her like the Eucharist. Another important aspect that some women mystics share with heretics is quietism, or the belief that once a certain state of spiritual ascent is achieved, i.e., a certain "quiet," one is incapable of sinning. Angela states this quite unequivocally in the seventh supplementary step: "when my soul sees His presence, it cannot commit any offense, and it receives many divine gifts" (74). She even claims that "while I am in this truth, I take equal delight when I see or understand a devil or adultery, as when I see or understand a good angel or a good deed" (74).

So in the opinion of several contemporary critics it is definitely time to abandon the traditional view of mysticism as a highly private, subjective, and ultimately ineffable experience, since this is a questionable perspective which tries to domesticate, seal, and ultimately silence women's spirituality even as it separates it from any ideal of social justice and therefore empties it of its political impact. Mysticism should be seen instead as a highly structured public discourse that was and is communal, dialogic, and active. In this way, disciplines that were originally designed to regulate and control the body (and we can think of the many ways mystics and anchorites have mortified their flesh through the centuries) are taken up and manipulated by the woman mystic as a method of self-determination (however ambivalent and, often, self-destructive), as a way of inscribing power on her own body.[7] Not surprisingly, such behaviors occur more frequently among women than among men in cultures

---

[7]   Laurie Finke argues this point very well in her essay "Mystical Bodies and the Dialogics of Vision," in *Maps of Flesh and Light: The Religious Experience of Medieval Women Mystics*, ed. Ulrike Wiethaus (Syracuse, NY: Syracuse University Press, 1993): 28–44.

where women are associated with self-sacrifice and service. This power and authority, together with those granted by visionary experience, then spill over from the body into other realms: speaking and being heard, leading and advising, healing the sick as well as founding convents and hospitals. Bodily asceticism, paramystical phenomena, and visionary experience are thus necessary in order to legitimate the woman writer and, especially, the woman saint, in the face of her institutional silencing. And, as I discuss in the next section of this Introduction, silent is just what these women, Angela among them, were not.

3. Angela's writings and spirituality: the *Memorial*

Mystical literature is often described as an oxymoron, for common sense demands that the experience of what goes beyond language cannot be verbalized. Yet, if mystical experience were truly ineffable, as numerous mystics and critics have repeatedly claimed, then the vast majority of non-mystics would have no access to it, for the evidence of mysticism is constituted for most of us by texts alone. And these texts, as anyone familiar with them knows, are long, often even prolix, and frequently characterized by their authors' skill in linguistic usage. Hence the paradox of the very expression "mystical language": etymologically, mysticism refers to that about which we cannot speak, and mystics – Angela among them – frequently lament the inadequacy of referential language to express their union with the divinity: one critic has counted fifty-one such protestations in Angela of Foligno alone.[8] Paradoxically, however, what we witness is the proliferation of the mystic's speech, her repeated attempt, through the negation of the capacities of language, to express the inexpressible. If it is primarily through their visionary experience that medieval holy women could claim spiritual (but also political) power and authority, then clearly such experience had to be communicable in everyday language. The inadequacy of language is fought by stretching language to its limits, by pulling it to the point of blasphemy, beyond every boundary of quotidian usage. Instead of receding into the background of ineffability, language becomes in the hands of the mystic an exuberant weapon. Angela's was not a privatized spirituality limited to the domestic and/or psychological sphere. And in order to assess the origin of and motives for its impact we need to study closely her text.

---

[8] Tiziana Arcangeli, "Re-reading a Mis-known and Mis-read Mystic: Angela da Foligno," *Annali d'italianistica* 13 (1995): 41–78, 69.

The most authoritative manuscript of Angela's writings is found in the Biblioteca Comunale of Assisi, and it is simply titled *Liber Lelle*, or "The book of Lella" – an almost mysterious appellation which rightly presages a difficult, unseizable, undefinable text. The best-known Latin title is longer and more specific: *Liber de vere fidelium experientia*, or "The book of the experience of the truly faithful." The first printed edition of Angela's writings dates from 1497, and since then the work has been repeatedly issued both in Latin and in many other languages. But it is only at the beginning of this century that critical editions have been undertaken by competent scholars, while formerly all editors were following a faulty fourteenth-century manuscript. At present, the most reliable version available is the critical edition published in 1985 by Ludger Thier and Abele Calufetti, which includes the Latin and a medieval Italian vernacular version, and on which this edition and translation is based.

The theoretical issues raised by the notion of the inexpressibility of the mystical experience are aggravated by the practical questions of the manuscripts and editions, and, more important, the very authorship of Angela's *Memorial*. I will not examine in this context the other half of Angela's *Liber*: the thirty-six *Instructions*, made up of texts of various genres, including letters, and the *Transition*, namely the account of Angela's final illness and death. These texts, with the possible exception of two Instructions, were not even dictated by Angela but rather were compiled by a number of anonymous writers.

As was the case for the majority of medieval women mystics, Angela did not write the *Memorial* with her own hand, and it is an arduous task to disentangle her voice from that of her scribe and confessor. On the other hand, without the latter's mediation we may never have heard Angela's voice, however filtered. And in the history of Italian women's mysticism, only the incomparably weaker voices of Chiara of Assisi (1193–1253) and Beatrice of Este (1200–1226) precede Angela's own, for the story of every other holy woman before Angela has reached us through hagiographers' legends rather than first-person revelations.

It is believed by most scholars that as Angela dictated in her Umbrian dialect, her scribe hastily translated and wrote everything down in a scholastic Latin that is often grammatically and syntactically incorrect and open to many vernacular intrusions. (Other scholars, however, maintain that the scribe must have compiled the text in the vernacular first and only later translated it into Latin.) The *Memorial* was composed in four to six years, from 1291 or 1292 until, probably, 1296 or 1297, when the text was ecclesiastically approved by Cardinal Giacomo Colonna and a number of other anonymous Franciscan theologians. Even in its Latin translation the reader can experience Angela's language as characterized by a lively, elementary syntax that clearly reflects the spoken word: her words are unadorned, her syntax is paratactical, or made up of short, juxtaposed sentences simply linked together by conjunctions and relative pronouns. Furthermore, Angela's frequent use of the passive form underlines this author's relative lack of control over her spiritual experience, her submission to the Other, her loss of her self in God.

The *Memorial* is divided into nine chapters, chronologically arranged to follow the twenty-six steps of Angela's spiritual journey, which had begun in 1285. *Passus* is the Latin term for "step" used in the *Memorial*, and at the beginning of the text the choice of the concept is attributed to Angela herself, rather than to the scribe. The first twenty steps of Angela's *Memorial*, which follow the purgative and illuminative way, are marked by poverty and the progressive shedding of all earthly possessions, characteristic of Franciscan spirituality. The remaining steps, on the other hand, are joined together by the motif of the journey – underlined by the term "passus," which indicates precisely a path, though a spiritual one. In the first six steps Angela is purified through suffering and the gift of penitential tears. This experience leads to confession and shame, but also to self-knowledge and the love of God. Steps seven to seventeen are distinguished by painful visions of the Crucified which intensify Angela's bond of desire to Jesus Christ as her lover. She sheds all of her clothes and all of her possessions, overcoming the shame and fear of begging, and offers herself completely to Christ, even as she continues her harsh penitential practices. Angela participates in the pain of Mary and Saint John at the foot of the cross, as well as in Christ's own suffering, and begins to feel the first delight of God's love in the sixteenth step. It is in the seventeenth step that Angela's entrance into the mystical state, the transcendental realm, is self-consciously definitive: this step marks the passage to the unitive stage through Angela's self-burial in Christ's Passion. The eighteenth and nineteenth steps are characterized by an increase of the fire of love and subsequent paranormal phenomena: extended fasting, uncontrollable shrieking, loss of speech, and mystical trance. The twentieth step coincides with Angela's encounter with God during her pilgrimage to Assisi. The actual period of time in which Angela remained in each of the first twenty steps cannot be established, though they altogether lasted approximately six years.

Because of his inability to accurately distinguish them from one another, the remaining eleven steps are condensed and renamed by the scribe as the seven supplementary steps, longer and more elaborate than the previous ones. The first one of these coincides with the last part of the twentieth step, hence the total number of twenty-six steps. (The scribe must thus change his initial statement that Angela's experience would take place in the course of thirty steps.) The supplementary steps describe Angela's heightened perception of Christ's Passion, namely her own reenactment of the mystery of the cross. As was also the case for other medieval mystics, Angela's focus on the Passion was linked with bridal mysticism and nurtured by the flowering of a genre of religious literature and imagery that expounded and expanded on the gospel narratives of Christ's agony and death. Yet unlike other women mystics who were her contemporaries, Angela does not experience the cross as the content of a vision but rather as a physical as well as spiritual part of herself, as belonging therefore to her very substance.

In the first supplementary step, Angela is courted by God and has a vision of Christ's beautiful throat and eyes. In the second supplementary step, she sees God as goodness and beauty, experiencing divine presence as love; God significantly blesses her at the moment of the elevation of the host. The next step contains both direct and indirect descriptions of God as food. The fourth supplementary step includes diabolic temptations, joy at the visions of the crucified body, and confirmation of God's love for Angela. The joy of participating in Christ's crucifixion begins in the fifth step to be accompanied by pain. Angela has visions of Christ's and Mary's poverty, of kissing and embracing Christ in the sepulchre, of divine love approaching her as a sickle, yet the harmony between body and soul which Angela describes in this very step leads to visible physical effects (her face becomes white and radiant) which her companion finds embarrassing when the two women are in public.

Before the perfect mystical union with God experienced in the seventh step, the pinnacle of her ascent to the divine ("You are I and I am you," Angela exclaims, 69), recounted in terms of divine darkness and characterized by repeated ecstasies, Angela must undergo the devastating moral and physical suffering of another, most horrible darkness – known in mystical literature as the dark night of the soul. During this time, Angela shared Christ's agony and abandonment on the cross. This period lasted about two years, and is recorded in the sixth supplementary step. At the end of the dark night, Angela realizes that suffering was needed for the purification of her soul. But Angela's mystical encounter with God in the seventh supplementary step is also an encounter with darkness, although of a kind different from the horrible darkness necessary for purification. It is an encounter characterized by affectivity rather than knowledge, it is a fall into the abyss of non-love, of pure negativity. In the end, Angela discovers that she resides within God. This theme of divine darkness is the aspect of Angela's spirituality that most clearly differs from Saint Francis's own; for at the apex of his mystical experience Francis finds the parental relationship of God the Father and God the Son, while Angela is plunged into an undescribable abyss reminiscent of Pseudo-Dionysius the Areopagite (a corpus of sixth-century spiritual writings which may have indirectly reached Angela): God is the human Christ, but God is also inaccessible darkness.

Angela's mystical path is far from being a straightforward one, and not only because of the oscillating vicissitudes, between doubt and certitude, for instance, of Angela's journey to God. The presence of the scribe in the course of the *Memorial* is far from being a self-effacing one, leading the reader to wonder about his actual role in the composition of the text. This is a chatty scribe who regularly interpolates his own comments, including candid and contradictory statements concerning both his faithfulness to Angela's words and his inability to transmit Angela's message accurately because of his ineptitude and deficiencies as a transcriber. Clearly, if we are to believe the former set of statements, we should also lend some credence to the latter: the scribe's lack of understanding of Angela's narrative must have influenced his presentation of it. Most obvious, for instance, is the problem of a shifting narrative perspective: the *Memorial* is sometimes told in the first person, Angela's own, and at other times in the third person, the scribe's.

Significantly, it was the scribe who compelled Angela to narrate her experiences to him, as a response to his own spiritual doubts and interests. This was rather common for holy women at that time. Angela, for her part, had little trouble obliging him, and even told him that the single sheet of paper he showed up with on their first day of writing would not suffice and that he would need a large notebook instead (36). It has also been hypothesized, for example, that it is because of the scribe's own spiritual uncertainties that Angela's vacillations between belief and doubt are so emphasized in the *Memorial*, and more generally, that the scribe's personal interests may have directed what he chose to eliminate and to include, what to condense and what to elaborate.[9] He admits to such selections in passing remarks. Bodily suffering, for instance, characteristic of medieval women's piety in general and certainly of Angela's own, is often alluded to in the *Memorial* yet it plays a relatively moderate role in the narrative.

The *Memorial* could then be seen as a collaborative effort, in the course of which Angela's spiritual experiences, orally expressed, are turned by her scribe into a material, written text. This relationship between holy woman penitent and male confessor was prominent during the Middle Ages, and it was also mutually beneficial for the couple involved: if the priest was attracted by the woman's example of living faith, her gift of prophecy, her intercessory role with God, and her active and original – even, at times, transgressive – teachings, the woman needed a priest's official approval and guidance as well as his ability to administer the sacraments – above all, the Eucharist, devotion to which was the most prominent concern of women's spirituality in the thirteenth century. This devotional choice by women was at least in part motivated by the fact that women could not have direct access to Holy Communion: they could only be recipients of it, rather than the ones who could consecrate it. At the same time, it is holy women who have the special role of unmasking, through eucharistic miracles, the clergy unworthy of consecrating the host. We see an instance of this in the *Memorial* itself: "when the priest who was celebrating Mass was ready for the consecration, she heard God say to her: 'There are many who break me and draw blood from my back.' And she saw and understood that the Host, which the priest had just broken, was speaking to her. After thinking about this, Christ's faithful one prayed these words: 'May he not be one of those.' And God said in response, 'He will never be one of those' " (71).

Echoing the scribe's own contradictions, Angela claims both that his redaction is weak and flavorless and that it contains nothing false or superfluous. Medieval religious authorship can be seen as a dialogic practice lacking the individualistic bent of modern writings. The dynamic interplay between Angela and her scribe underlines the cultural exchange between female and male, lay and cleric, sole protagonist and primary narrator. This relationship intrinsically critiques

---

9   Catherine M. Mooney, "The Authorial Role of Brother A. in the Composition of Angela of Foligno's *Revelations*," in *Creative Women in Medieval and Early Modern Italy: A Religious and Artistic Renaissance*, ed. E. Ann Matter and John Coakley (Philadelphia: University of Pennsylvania Press, 1994): 34–63, 49.

the romantic notion of authorship that has been more recently undermined from various ideological perspectives (Marxist, feminist, deconstructionist, to name a few). Its complexity could then be seen by the contemporary reader in an optimistic light, as the source of understanding rather than confusion, of jubilation rather than dismay.

Angela of Foligno's *Memorial* expresses, according to some critics, the highest mystical voice of a medieval Italian woman.[10] Angela's itinerary goes through the three stages of love, nothingness, and resurrection, always through the body – her own, Christ's – and through the cross. Ineffability is what mystical language translates into the space of human knowledge and communication. It does not simply indicate silence as the inability to speak. Rather, ineffability is a stage, albeit a paradoxical one, in the mystic's journey. This journey is both spiritual and embodied and it is expressed through a poetics of vision. If visionary experience legitimates Angela's authority and action, then visionary language constitutes Angela's very text. Hers is an excessive, transgressive language, one that self-consciously goes beyond the limits of what can/should be said about God. Hence, first of all, Angela's frequent statements, throughout the *Memorial*, concerning the blasphemous and at the same time, paradoxically, the true nature of her speech: the inadequacy of human language in expressing the mystic's encounter with the divine translates itself not into silence – so much for ineffability – but rather into linguistic excess. This excess manifests itself both in terms of quantity and, more important, in terms of quality: Angela's language goes beyond sanctioned devotional and doctrinal models. It is a language that hovers or is divided between absolute truth and deceptive, even mendacious blasphemy, just as, in the attempt to overcome ineffability, her words vertiginously move towards becoming, themselves, part of the mystical experience. There is much more at stake here than the scribe's complaint that what Angela says is not found in the Scriptures.

Angela's excesses are not confined to the linguistic sphere, nor to the spiritual realm: these two become transgressively intertwined

---

10 Pozzi and Leonardi refer to Angela's "mystical consciousness" as "undoubtedly the highest of all Italian medieval women"; Giovanni Pozzi and Claudio Leonardi, eds., *Scrittrici mistiche italiane* (Genova: Marietti, 1988), 136. Rosamaria Lavalva writes of Angela's "mystical madness" that it was "perhaps the most sublime expressed by an Italian woman of the Middle Ages." "The Language of Vision in Angela da Foligno's *Liber de vera* [sic] *fidelium experientia*," *Stanford Italian Review* 11.1–2 (1992): 103–122, 107.

with her unconventional religious practices. Angela's most notorious episode of this sort, which took place on Holy Thursday of 1292, is her washing of a leper's sores, followed by her drinking of the water used for the ablution. When a scab gets stuck in her throat, it tastes to her as if she had taken communion. This episode reveals both Angela's transgression (the act goes beyond human solidarity to the point of disgust, and anyway Angela does not, indeed may not have the power to consecrate anything) and her conformity to the eucharistic devotion of thirteenth-century women. For Angela, as for other medieval holy women, images of eating and non-eating (fasting and feasting, in the evocative words of the title of Caroline Walker Bynum's best-known work) were central, and in their complexity these images cannot possibly be reduced to what we today call anorexia – even though they share some of the aspects of anorexia.[11] Because if on the one hand food had to be rejected as part of the material filth of this world, still food was also, quite literally, God through the Eucharist and the miracle of transubstantiation – the transformation, through consecration, of bread and wine into the body and blood of Christ. The bodily and the spiritual are forever intertwined in this Christian doctrine which, by the way, women's eucharistic miracles served to support and confirm (eucharistic miracles involved the visible transformation of the Host – in the tabernacle, on the paten, in the priest's hands – into Christ).

The constant mutual influence of body and spirit is indeed one of the most salient features of Angela's writings, and I return to this subject in the interpretive essay that follows the selection from the *Memorial.* Be it the erotic body or the maternal body, the eating and feeding body or the suffering and dying body, corporeality, and, more specifically, female corporeality, is central to Angela's experience of the divine: if the Host is more savory for Angela than any other food, it also makes her tremble violently. And Christ's presence in her soul, for example, makes her very joints dislocate noisily (61). Her human, woman's body encounters Christ's divine one, and it is only through this union, corporeal as well as spiritual, that she is capable of achieving a total *imitatio Christi,* a physical and spiritual imitation of Christ.

---

[11] On this subject, see Caroline Walker Bynum, *Holy Feast and Holy Fast: The Religious Significance of Food to Medieval Women* (Berkeley: University of California Press, 1987); Rudolph Bell, *Holy Anorexia* (Chicago: University of Chicago Press, 1985).

4. The legacy of Angela of Foligno

In spite of her enormous popularity during and immediately follow-ing her lifetime (although Angela is often referred to as "santa," she was never canonized), Angela of Foligno has been largely excluded from the standard classics of Italian literature. This is in part because the *Memorial* was not written in the Tuscan vernacular, Italy's liter-ary language, in part because Angela's style, like that of the women mystics who were her contemporaries, does not fit into those aesthetic and ideological parameters which define our notion of liter-ature. Furthermore, the early dissemination of the *Memorial* may have been hindered by the fact that it was officially approved by the powerful yet controversial Cardinal Giacomo Colonna, who sympa-thized with the Spirituals (the more extreme branch of the followers of Saint Francis) and was excommunicated by Boniface VIII shortly after having signed his approval of the text. In fact, we do not even know the names of the other eight Franciscan theologians who signed the approbation with Cardinal Colonna, nor of the other three that signed it later (an anonymity likely tied to the cultural perception of Angela's book as suspect). From a more recent perspective, Angela of Foligno's works have usually been issued by publishers affiliated with religious orders. An important exception to this rule is the anthology edited by the noted scholar of spirituality Giovanni Pozzi and published by the Italian high-brow house Adelphi in 1992 as *Il libro dell'esperienza*, or The book of experience. Finally, the very textual reliability of most editions of Angela's writings has been questioned, even though the large number of extant manuscripts and their broad-ranging dissemination point to the fact that her texts have been widely read over the centuries.

From very early on, Angela's writings were more widely dissemi-nated abroad than they were in Italy, and it is therefore not surprising that even in the course of our present century Angela should have exerted a more powerful influence in France than in her own country. This influence was spurred by Ernest Hello's (1828–1885) im-mensely inaccurate yet highly poetic and popular French translation, first published in 1868 and entitled *Le livre des visions et instructions de la bienheureuse Angèle de Foligno*. Thus she is quoted by French Catholic writers as different as Joris-Karl Huysmans (1848–1907) and Georges Bernanos (1888–1948), in *En route* (1895) and *Dialogues of the Carmelites* (1949) respectively. Still her most con-spicuous and surprising presence in twentieth-century literature can be found in the transgressive oeuvre of Georges Bataille (1897–1962), characterized by an implacable analysis of human perversions and a fascination with mystical experience. Angela for example dominates Bataille's *Guilty* (1944), a fragmentary World War II journal in which her life and visions, mediated by Hello's translation, constitute a model for the atheistic narrator's attempt to attain mystical ecstasy – a form of pleasure deemed possible even in the absence of a belief in God, and which the narrator takes great pains to distinguish from erotic bliss. Angela of Foligno is posited in this text as both an existential and a linguistic model, as a master of radical, transgressive human experience and of its only apparently ineffable verbal representation.

That Angela of Foligno's writings continue to be relevant to intellectual and spiritual history is clear. And one of the most interesting findings of a contemporary re-reading of her work is the continuity between her spiritual, existential, and linguistic concerns and those experienced by many twentieth-century women. Even though there may be considerable disagreement, and even though women like Angela were far from conforming to our idea of what constitutes a feminist, still so many of the questions asked by medieval mystics and by contemporary women are strikingly analogous. This is not only true within the Christian tradition, when we look at the issues raised by modern women mystics as diverse as Gemma Galgani (1878–1903) in Italy and Simone Weil (1909–1943) in France. For it can be argued that mystical theology has explored the realm of human interiority more extensively, more in depth, and certainly for a longer time than any other discipline (such as psychology and psychoanalysis). Thus, Angela's questioning presence has also had an impact among a very different and influential group of women: French feminist theorists. In her seminal work *The Second Sex* (1949), for example, Simone de Beauvoir repeatedly (and critically) cites Angela of Foligno in order to underline the erotomaniac nature of mysticism and its paralyzing relegation of woman to a self-destructive relationship with an unreality – God.

But the more recent work of psychoanalytic theorists Julia Kristeva and Luce Irigaray is less simplistic and, although not religious, more sympathetic to the claims of Christian women mystics. According to Luce Irigaray's *Speculum of the Other Woman* (1974), mysticism and femininity, inseparably intertwined, are places that subvert the patriarchal order. Mystical discourse allows women's speech to become public, to articulate female language through an excess of both body and words. Angela of Foligno is quoted by Irigaray in an epigraph to her chapter "La mystérique" (which abounds in Angelan echoes throughout) in order to underscore mystical eroticism as a peculiarly female pleasure that allows the convergence, in mystical union, of the divinity and the woman's flesh. Finally, Julia Kristeva's *Powers of Horror* (1980) describes Christian mysticism as one of the most important modalities of the abject, i.e., the object of primary repression, the horror of undecidability. The episode I briefly discussed above of Angela of Foligno's drinking of the water used to wash a leper's sore is presented by Kristeva as an example of the *jouissance* (an untranslatable word that can refer both to extreme pleasure and to sexual orgasm) that alone allows the subject to have access to the "real." In self-abjection the mystic finds a pleasure that is distinct from masochism, as well as the ability to transgress boundaries: between spirit and flesh, between words and the ineffable.

The central questions shared by Angela of Foligno and contemporary feminist thought, then, include the possibility/impossibility of representing the body through verbal language, and the role played by this same body in the acquisition of knowledge. Knowledge of both self and God is indeed absolutely central to Angela's experience and writings, and it constitutes an important part of practically every single step of her *Memorial*. Both medieval women mystics and contemporary feminists underline, in their practice and/or in their theory, the potential of women's association with corporeality in terms of their acquisition of knowledge – women's ability, that is, to attain and to express knowledge in and through their bodies. This association, it should be noted, is equally debased by the more or less overt misogyny of medieval theology and of modern positivistic medicine. For the medieval mystic, and certainly for Angela, embodiment is necessary for redemption, as well as for one's own knowledge of such redemption – a personal necessity theologically grounded in the redemption of humanity through the Incarnation of God in Christ. This knowledge is in turn based on the awareness of self and other, of woman and God, of sin and virtue, of greatness and poverty, of love and nothingness. For the contemporary feminist, gendered embodiment is the sign of difference and its *jouissance*, and it is the prelude to emancipation through knowledge of self and other, of body and/as words.

The *Memorial*
of Angela of Foligno

Prologue[1]

Concerning the Incarnate Word of Life, the experience of the truly faithful proves concretely what the Lord Himself says in the Gospel: "Whoever loves me will keep my word, and my Father will love him and we will come to him and make our home within him." And He says: "Whoever loves me . . . I will reveal myself to him."[2]

God Himself allows His faithful ones to fully demonstrate this experience and the teachings derived from it. Recently God has again allowed one of His faithful to authenticate this experience and its teachings, in order to increase the devotion of His people. What follows describes these things in words which are incomplete and inadequate, and yet they are nonetheless true.

Why and how I, an unworthy scribe, was compelled by God (as I believe) to write, and how this faithful one of Christ was completely compelled to speak, will be found below, where I explain when I began to know of and to write about these things.[3]

The First Twenty Steps

A certain woman faithful to Christ said that, while speaking with her companion about God, she had discerned within herself thirty steps or changes which the soul makes as it proceeds along the path of penance.[4]

The first step is a knowledge of sin, which makes the soul very much afraid of being damned to Hell. There is bitter crying at this step.

---

[1] The prologue is preceded in three important Latin manuscripts by a short text entitled "testificatio" (declaration or testimony), which testifies that the *Memorial* was approved by Cardinal Giacomo Colonna (d.1318) before his excommunication by Pope Boniface VIII in 1296 (he was reinstated nine years later by Clement V), and by many other examiners – who unanimously judged it to be a holy book.

[2] These are references to the Gospel of John, 14:23 and 14:21. References to God as "He," although somewhat distasteful to feminist sensibilities, are an integral part of Angela's spirituality and need to be translated literally.

[3] On the scribe and his interpolations, see the Introduction, pp. 10–15.

[4] This sentence shows that the term *passus*, or step, central to Angela's self-understanding and to the *Memorial*, was in fact her own (and not the scribe's) choice. The division of the soul's ascent into a numerical sequence was a practice quite common during the medieval period, and it frequently patterned itself after John Climacus's *Ladder of Paradise* or *Ladder of Divine Ascent*. On Angela's companion, see the Introduction, p. 2.

The second step is a confession of sin accompanied by shame and bitterness. At this point the soul feels no love, only pain. She told me how she often received communion while still in a state of sin, because she was too ashamed to make a full confession. Day and night her conscience kept nagging her. And then she asked Blessed Francis to find her a confessor who would know her sins, someone to whom she could make a good confession; that same night the old friar appeared to her and said, "Sister, if you had asked me sooner, I would have acted sooner on your behalf; in any case, what you have asked for has been accomplished."[5]

"And in the morning I went immediately to the Church of Saint Francis, and then I quickly returned.[6] On my way home I entered the Cathedral of Saint Felician and found a friar preaching; he was the chaplain of the bishop.[7] Immediately, at the Lord's urging, I decided to make a full confession to him, provided that he had the authority of the bishop to absolve me, or that he could get the bishop himself to absolve me. I made a good confession to him. After hearing it, he said that if I was not satisfied, he would report all my sins to the bishop; he also said, 'I will inform you of the penance which the bishop will impose, even though I myself can absolve you without the bishop.'" At this step the soul still experiences shame and bitterness, and feels no love, only pain.

The third step is the penance which is performed in order to make reparation with God for sins; there is still much pain.

The fourth step is an awareness of the divine mercy which has freed the soul from Hell. At this point the soul begins to be enlightened. Then there is more crying and pain than before; the soul also strives to perform a more severe penance.

---

[5] The "old friar" refers quite likely to Francis of Assisi himself.

[6] This is the first of many switches the scribe makes from narration in the third person when the scribe recounts Angela's experience, to first-person narration, in which the scribe lets Angela speak of herself. The scribe mentions these inconsistencies. In spite of the difficulties they pose to the reader, it is important to preserve these incongruities in the translation into English: in addition to conveying the style of the Latin text, this practice is a constant reminder of the dialogic manner of writing that is central to the redaction of the *Memorial*, and of the difficulties encountered by Angela in making her voice known as mystic, as writer, and as woman.

The Church of Saint Francis in Foligno is where the encounters of Angela with her scribe took place. It is also in this church that Angela was buried.

[7] For many scholars, this passage documents Angela's first encounter with her scribe and confessor. There is, however, no documentary proof that the scribe and the friar mentioned here are in fact the same person.

I, brother scribe, state that I did not write about the amazing penance which this faithful one of Christ was performing, because I learned about it after I had already recorded these steps. She did not at the time reveal her penance to me except as it was necessary to distinguish between the different steps. I was willing to write down only what she told me. In fact, I omitted much that I was not able to write.

The fifth step is self-knowledge.[8] Now somewhat enlightened, the soul sees in itself nothing but defects. It then condemns itself before God because it most certainly deserves Hell. Here also there is bitter crying.

"And you should understand that each of these steps lasts for a period of time. It is very pitiful and a cause of great heartache that the soul can move itself in the direction of God only very slowly and painfully in order to advance a very small step. As for myself I know that I lingered and wept at every step.[9] I was not allowed to advance all at once, although there was some consolation for me in my tears – but it was a bitter consolation.

The sixth step is a kind of illuminating grace which gave me a profound knowledge of all my sins. And in that illumination I saw that I had offended all the creatures that were made for me. And in a profound way all my sins were brought back into my memory as I was confessing them before God.[10] And I begged all the creatures, which I saw I had offended, not to accuse me. Then an intense fire of love moved me to pray. And I called on all the saints and the Blessed Virgin to intercede for me and to beg the Love which had already done so many good things for me to make me live – because I knew that I was now dead. And it seemed to me that all the creatures and all the saints took pity on me.

At the seventh step I was moved to reflect on the cross where I saw that Christ had died for us. Although the vision was still without flavor, it was accompanied by great pain.[11]

---

[8] The belief in self-knowledge as fundamental to spiritual life was widespread among medieval writers. Its basic source was found in Saint Augustine's *Confessions*, and it was developed, for example, in the works of Saint Bernard and Saint Bonaventure.

[9] In this paragraph there is an abrupt grammatical shift in person and tense: from third to first person and from present tense to past. Until now the text seemed to focus on a general program for the soul, while at this point Angela's personal experience is recounted.

[10] As the means for retrieving one's past sins, memory plays a recurrent and important role in Angela's spiritual life.

[11] This step documents Angela's first important encounter with the cross, which was to become the center of her spiritual development.

At the eighth step, while looking at the cross, I was given a deeper understanding of how the Son of God had died for our sins. And with extreme pain I again became aware of all my sins – I felt that I myself had crucified Him. But I still did not know which was the greater good: that He had rescued me from my sins and from hell and converted me to penance, or that He had been crucified for me. But together with this understanding of the cross I was given such a fire that, as I was standing near the cross, I stripped myself of all my clothes, and offered myself completely to Him.[12] And although I was afraid, I promised to observe perpetual chastity and not to offend Him with any part of my body. I also accused every part of my body, one at a time, before Him. And I asked Him to make me observe the chastity of all my body parts and all my senses; I was afraid to make this promise, but at the same time, that fire compelled me, and I could not do otherwise.

At the ninth step I was moved to seek the way of the cross, so that I could stay at the foot of the cross, where all sinners take refuge. And the way of the cross was illuminated, demonstrated, and taught to me in the following way – that is, it was revealed to me that if I wanted to go to the cross, I should strip myself, become lighter, and go naked to the cross; in other words, I should forgive everyone who has offended me and strip myself of everything earthly including, all men, women, friends, and relatives, and all other things, such as my possessions; I should even strip away my own self; and I should give my heart to Christ who had accomplished so much good for me; and finally, I should proceed along the path of thorns, that is, the path of tribulation.

And then I began to reject fine foods, fancy clothing and head-dresses. But there was still shame and sorrow, because I did not yet feel any love. And I was still with my husband – and so there was bitterness when I was spoken to or treated unjustly; nevertheless, I

---

[12] The stripping in front of the Crucifix – literal in this step, metaphorical in the next – is an important event in Angela's journey. She imitates Saint Francis, who reportedly stripped himself naked before everybody in the town square of Assisi. But her gesture is also related to the heretical practice of praying naked in imitation of Adam and Eve before the Fall. Furthermore, the theme of spiritual nudity was common in medieval times, especially among Spiritual Franciscans, as symbolic of the radical poverty exemplified by Christ. Angela's gesture was nevertheless audacious and downright scandalous, exemplary of her willingness to break human rules in order to follow God.

endured as patiently as I could.[13] And then in accordance with God's will, my mother died; she had been a great hindrance to me. Later, my husband and all my children died within a short time. And because I had already begun the way of the cross and had asked God that they should die, I felt a deep consolation following their deaths.[14] I knew that God had accomplished these things for me, and that my heart would always be in God's heart and God's heart would always be in mine.

At the tenth step, when I was asking God what I could do to better please Him, He took pity on me and often appeared to me, both when I was asleep and awake; each time, he appeared hanging on the cross. He told me that I should look at His wounds. And in a wonderful way He showed me how He endured all this for me. This happened many times. And after He showed me all that He endured – each thing one at a time – for my sake, He said to me, 'What, then, can you do in return which would be sufficient?' He appeared to me many times like this – more pleasantly when I was awake than when I slept – although He always appeared to be suffering greatly, and He spoke to me (as He had when I slept) showing all His wounds from His feet to His head. He even showed me the hairs of His beard, eyebrows, and head, which had been plucked out; and He counted every blow of the whip, pointing to each one, and then He said, 'All this I endured for you.'[15]

And all my sins were brought back to my memory in a wonderful way, and I was shown that since I had again recently wounded Him with my sins, I should feel extreme pain. And I then experienced greater pain for my sins than ever before. And again as I was watching His Passion, He said, 'What can you do for me in return which would be sufficient?' Then I was crying and weeping so feverishly that the tears began to burn my flesh; later, I had to cool my skin with water.

At the eleventh step, because of what I just said, I pushed myself to perform harsher penance." This is a long step. And her penance

---

[13] Angela does not specify who spoke and acted unjustly towards her. It was probably her husband who mistreated her. This would help explain the curious fact that he is conspicuously missing from the list of family members whose death caused Angela great sorrow. See p. 44.

[14] I have discussed in the Introduction and the Interpretive Essay the significance of this remarkable prayer. See pp. 1–2 and 83–84.

[15] Counting the afflictions suffered by Christ in the course of his Passion was a common theme among medieval women mystics. Other common themes that appear in this part of the *Memorial* include sharing the pain of John and Mary at the Cross (thirteenth and fifteenth steps), drinking at the wound on Christ's side, and desiring a comparably reviled death (fourteenth step).

was wonderful and difficult beyond ordinary human capability, as I, brother scribe, later learned.[16]

"At the twelfth step, when I realized that I could not perform adequate penance while in the company of the things of this world, I resolved to completely leave everything, so that I could do penance and come to the cross, as God had inspired me to do. Moreover, this resolution was a gift from God given by His wonderful grace in the following way: When I strongly desired to become poor, I kept thinking zealously that I must not die before I become poor. On the other hand, I knew I would be assaulted by many trials; since I was young, begging could be dangerous as well as shameful for me. Still I thought I should die of hunger, cold, and nakedness. And when everyone was trying to dissuade me from this, then merciful God in His own time sent a great illumination into my heart. This illumination brought with it a kind of strength which I did not think I would ever lose – I still do not think I will ever lose it. In that illumination I thought and decided that: If I ought to die of hunger or nakedness or shame, and if this pleased or could possibly please God, then I could not possibly dismiss these things, even if I were certain that I would suffer all these ills – because even if I did suffer all these ills, I would die happy with respect to God. And from that time on I was truly resolved to become poor.

At the thirteenth step, I entered into the pain of the Mother of Christ and of Saint John,[17] and I asked them to obtain for me the certainty of a sign so that I could always be mindful of Christ's Passion. Soon after, while I was sleeping, the Heart of Christ appeared to me and I was told, 'In this Heart there is nothing false; everything there is true.'[18] I thought this happened to me because I had made fun of a certain preacher.[19]

---

[16] The *Memorial* does not specify what sort of penance Angela performed, but the more common forms for medieval recluses included: self-flagellation; standing for a long time barefoot, or on one foot, or with arms outstretched; multiple prostrations and genuflections; use of a hairshirt; fasting.

[17] This is Saint John the apostle and evangelist, who was often associated with the Virgin Mary in medieval devotion (a popular belief even held that he had ascended into heaven along with Mary). John was the only one of the twelve apostles to be present at Christ's crucifixion.

[18] The cult of the Heart of Christ appears only sporadically in Angela of Foligno, while it is central to the visionary experience of some of her contemporaries – such as Margherita of Cortona. In Angela's experience, Christ's wounded side is more important than his Sacred Heart.

[19] The name of this preacher remains unknown.

At the fourteenth step, while I was awake and praying, Christ showed Himself to me on the cross more clearly, that is, He gave me a greater knowledge of Himself. And then He summoned me and told me to place my mouth at the wound in His side; and it seemed to me that I was seeing and drinking His blood as it was freshly flowing from His side; and I was given to understand that with His blood He was cleansing me.[20] And here I began to have great joy, although I still experienced sorrow at the thought of His Passion.

And I asked God to let me pour out all my blood for His love just as He had done for me. And I was determined because of His love to want all the parts of my body to suffer a death more vile than His. And I kept thinking and wanting to find someone to kill me, provided I could be rightfully killed for faith in Him or love of Him; I would ask my killer that since Christ was crucified on a tree, he should crucify me in a ditch or in some vile place and in a most vile way. And because I was not worthy to die as saints die, I would ask my killer to make sure I died a long and vile death. And I was not able to think of a death as vile as I desired; in fact, it was very painful that I, completely unworthy to die as the saints die, could not find a vile death for myself.

At the fifteenth step, I reflected on the pain of Saint John and the Mother of God, and I asked them to obtain for me this grace: that I would always feel some of the pain of Christ's Passion, or at least some of their pain. They found and continue to find that grace for me. One time Saint John gave me more pain than I had ever felt. And I was given to understand that Saint John had endured such pain for the suffering and death of Christ as well as for the pain of Christ's Mother. For this reason I thought, and I still think, that Saint John was more than a martyr.

Then I was given such a strong desire to give away all my possessions, a desire which I could not possibly ignore, no matter what good or bad things might happen to me – even though a demon often assaulted me and tempted me not to do this, and even though this was forbidden by you,[21] as well as by all the other friars who used to counsel me. And if I had not been able to give away everything to the poor, I would have completely disowned all my possessions, because it seemed to me that I could not keep anything for myself without

---

[20] Many medieval women mystics drank at the wound on Christ's side. This action, associated with breastfeeding, is discussed further in the Interpretive Essay (pp. 93–95).

[21] The "you" to whom Angela refers is her scribe.

committing a serious offense. And still there was bitterness in my soul for my sins, and I did not know whether anything I did was pleasing to God. I began crying out with bitter weeping: 'Lord, even if I am already damned, I will still do penance, give away all that I have, and serve You.' And although I was still filled with bitterness for my sins, and still without divine sweetness, I was transformed from this condition in the following way.

During the sixteenth step, I once went to church and asked God for a certain grace. And while I was praying, He placed in my heart the 'Our Father' along with such a clear understanding of divine goodness and of my own unworthiness; every single word was explained to me in my heart. And I was reciting the 'Our Father' so slowly and with such self-knowledge that, although I was weeping bitterly for my sins and for my unworthiness, which I was becoming aware of in that prayer, nevertheless I experienced great consolation, and I began to have a taste of divine sweetness, because in that prayer better than anywhere else I was becoming aware of divine goodness. (I still find it there better than anywhere else.) But because my unworthiness and my sins were pointed out to me in that 'Our Father,' I began to be so ashamed that I hardly dared to raise my eyes; but I again appealed to the Blessed Virgin so that she might obtain for me forgiveness of my sins. And I was still full of bitterness for my sins.

And in each of these steps I remained for a time before I moved on to the next step; but in some steps I stayed longer, in others I stayed for a shorter time." That is why Christ's faithful one marveled and said, "O, the soul progresses so slowly – there is nothing written here about that! The soul is so strongly bound, as if with shackles on its feet, and it gets such evil assistance from the world and the devil."

"At the seventeenth step, after that, I was shown how the Blessed Virgin obtained for me the grace which gave me a different faith from what I had, because it seemed to me that until this step my faith was, by comparison, almost dead, and that the tears I had shed were, by comparison, almost forced out of me. Now I grieved more genuinely about Christ's Passion and about the pain of Christ's Mother. And then it seemed to me that whatever I did and however much I did it – it all seemed so inadequate to me. And I had the will to perform greater penance. So I enclosed myself in the Passion of Christ, and received the hope that there I could find freedom.

And then I began to receive consolation through dreams. I began having beautiful dreams, and was given consolation in them. And I began to receive sweetness from God within my soul continually – both while I was awake and while I was asleep. But because I still was not feeling certain of the origin of these experiences, that sweetness was mixed with bitterness, and I wanted something else from God."

And she reported to me one of her many dreams and visions. She said: "One time I was in my cell where I had shut myself for the Great Lent, and I was lovingly meditating on one passage from the Gospel – a passage of the greatest worth and of extreme delight.[22] I was next to the Missal, and had a strong thirst to see that passage in writing; fearing pride, although it was difficult, I restrained myself and kept from opening that book and giving in to an excessive thirst and love.[23] Then I grew sleepy and finally fell asleep still having this desire. Immediately I was led into a vision: I was told that an understanding of the Epistle was so delightful that anyone who understood it well would forget all worldly matters. And the one who was leading me said, 'Do you want to experience this?' And when I, intensely thirsty for this, said 'yes,' I was immediately led to this experience. And I was understanding divine goodness with such delight that I immediately forgot all worldly matters. And the one who was leading me told me that an understanding of the Gospel was so very delightful that anyone who understood it, would not only forget all worldly matters, but would also completely forget one's own self. And again the one leading me allowed me to experience this. And immediately I was understanding divine goodness with such delight that I completely forgot all worldly matters, and I completely forgot my self. I was in such divine delight that I asked the one who was leading me never to take me away from there. And I was told that what I was asking was not yet possible; and immediately I was led back. And I opened my eyes and felt the greatest joy from what I had seen, but I was very pained that I had lost it. The memory of this vision still delights me very much. From then on I had such certainty and light and such a burning love of God that I affirmed without a doubt that what is preached about the delight of God is nothing; those who preach are not able to preach that, nor do

---

22 The term "Great Lent" refers to the forty days which precede Easter, or what Christians today generally call Lent. The other Lents observed by medieval Christians took place during Advent and around Pentecost.

   The cell to which Angela refers ("carcer" is the Latin word) was probably the smallest and poorest room in the house. Many holy women voluntarily shut themselves in a similarly small and solitary space for the duration of Lent as a form of prayer and penance.

23 This passage seems to indicate that Angela knew how to read.

they understand what they do preach. The one who led me in this vision told me so.

At the eighteenth step, I experienced feelings of God, and I experienced such delight in prayer that I forgot about eating. And I wanted not to need to eat, so I could remain in prayer. But a certain temptation kept interfering: that I should not eat, or if I should eat, that I should eat very little. I knew this was a deception. Still, there was so much fire from the love of God in my heart that I did not grow tired from genuflecting or from any penance.

Later the fire became so great that if I heard any talk of God, I would start screeching. Even if someone had stood over me with an axe to kill me, I would not have been able to keep from screeching. This happened to me for the first time when I had sold my country house – the best property that I had – to give to the poor. And I used to mock Petruccio, but now I could not do that any more.[24] Also, when people told me that I was possessed by a demon, because I could not control myself, I became very ashamed and I began to agree that I was perhaps sick and possessed; I could not contradict those who spoke ill of me.

And whenever I saw the Passion of Christ depicted in art, I could not bear it; a fever would overtake me and I would become sick. For this reason, my companion carefully hid all pictures of the Passion from me.[25]

At the nineteenth step, after that period of screeching, and after that wonderful illumination and consolation which I experienced in reciting the 'Our Father,' I felt the first great consolation of God's sweetness in this way: Once I was inspired and drawn to consider the delight which there is in the contemplation of the divinity and the humanity of Christ. This resulted in a greater consolation than I had ever experienced, so that I stood for most of that day in my cell where I had been praying, confined and alone. After this experience I collapsed and lost the power of speech. Then my companion found me and thought that I was dying or on the verge of death, and that bothered me, because she was distracting me during that very intense consolation."

---

[24] This Pietruccio is the Blessed Pietro Crisci of Foligno, a contemporary of Angela (he died in 1323) who gave his possessions to the poor, became a Franciscan Tertiary, and lived as a recluse in the tower of the Cathedral of Foligno.

[25] Inordinately powerful effects of holy images on one's physical constitution were also common among women mystics of Angela's time.

Another time, before she had finished giving away all her possessions, although very little remained to be given, in the evening while
she was praying she said that she did not seem to be feeling God. She
was lamenting this and asked God, "Lord, I am only doing this so
that I may find you. Will I find you after I have finished?" She continued to pray for a long time. Then she received this response:
"What do you want?" She replied, "I don't want gold or silver; even
if you should give me the whole world, I don't want anything but
you." Then came this reply: "Finish what you have set out to do,
because immediately after you are done, the whole Trinity will come
into you."

"He made many other promises to me then, and freed me from all
tribulation before leaving me with much sweetness. And from then
on I looked forward to receiving what had been promised to me. And
then I told all this to my companion – though I had doubts because
too many great things had been promised to me; but, He had left me
with much divine sweetness.

Later, at the twentieth step, I went to the Church of Saint Francis in
Assisi. And on the way the promise made to me – the one I told you
about – was fulfilled, and I don't remember whether I had completed
giving everything away; in fact, no, I had not yet finished giving
everything to the poor.[26] Very little still remained, but a certain man
had told me to wait for him to return from Apulia, where he was
going to get some of his possessions from a brother who was in that
region; he said he would return immediately to give his entire portion
to the poor, at the same time that I did.[27] He wanted to give away all
his possessions at the same time as I did, since, by the grace of God,
it was at my admonition that he had been converted and was so
inspired. So I waited for him. But later I received a reliable report
that this man died during his journey, and that God caused miracles
through him, and that his tomb was revered."

The previous step, here called the twentieth, is the first that I, the
unworthy brother scribe, wrote, and it is the first that I had heard
related from the mouth of Christ's faithful one.[28] And I am not here

---

[26] The language and colloquial style of this sentence is a reminder of the oral origin
of Angela's text.

[27] We do not know the name of the man Angela is describing in this passage.

[28] It is at this stage of Angela's spiritual journey, namely as she begins the experiences of the first supplementary step, that she and the scribe meet. While the first
twenty steps have already occurred by then, the seven supplementary ones take
place in the same time frame as the dictation of the *Memorial*. The scribe is therefore also a personal witness to these final experiences.

going to complete this step which is very wonderful and full of divine revelation – it is also very long and delightful and full of divine intimacy, although the twenty-first step is even more wonderful. But I will wait to complete this step after I first relate briefly how, by the wonderful workings of Christ, I came to know of these things and how I was compelled to make a complete account of them.

First, it should be noted that I, brother scribe, with God's help was eager to continue with this project, from the first step all the way to the twenty-first, or to the end of the second revelation; there it is written that God, in a wonderful way, revealed to her that we had written the truth without any falsehood – although her account was much more complete, and I had shortened and diminished it in my writing.

But, in fact, I did not know how to continue this project from that point on, because I could speak with her for the purpose of writing only rarely and sporadically. Also, starting from the nineteenth step, I did not know for sure how to number and distinguish one step from the other.[29] So I have organized the remaining material under seven steps or revelations which coincide with the gifts of divine grace that I perceived that she had received, as well as her growth in those gifts and in the charisms of grace, which I had observed and learned about, and also as I thought more fitting and appropriate.

Scribe's Summary of the Seven Supplementary Steps[30]

The first step, which will be presented after an introduction, is the wonderful revelation of the intimacy, conversation, and teachings of God. The end of this step contains the response made to her about the Trinity, and how she saw Christ in the sacrament of the altar.

The second step is the revelation of the divine anointing, and of the vision of God in paradise. It also mentions that God requires the soul to love Him without malice; there follows a shortened version of

---

[29] With an interruption of his narration, the scribe changes at this point the initial division of Angela's *Memorial* into thirty steps. Rather, after describing the first nineteen steps, he decides to condense the remaining eleven ones into seven supplementary steps because, by his own admission, he does not know how to distinguish between and enumerate them. The first of these coincides with the twentieth step, hence a total of twenty-six rather than twenty-seven steps.

[30] What follows is an accurate, although very incomplete summary of the seven supplementary steps written by the scribe. It probably functioned as an index and was inserted in this place at the end of Angela's dictation.

what was a long address in which God reveals that He is the love of the soul; God wants the soul to have or to want to have something similar to the true love which God has shown in loving us. This step also teaches that every soul that wants to discover and receive divine mercy, can find it, just as Mary Magdalen did; this proceeds from the Father's love and goodness, and also from the sinner's recognition of His love and goodness; for these two reasons, the greater sinner is able to find greater mercy and grace. This step also mentions that God Himself is the love of the soul; also, Christ's faithful one received a revelation that she was pleasing to God, and that He was present in what we were writing, and that everything we had written was without falsehood. This step also includes how God – and later the Blessed Virgin – blessed the alms which she received. And finally it mentions the ecstasy experienced by her when she saw the body of Christ.

The third step is the revelation of divine instruction by way of teachings, some of which the ears of the body hear and others which are understood only by the tasting of the mind. This step teaches that the legitimate children of God are those who seek to know God, their Father, who gave them the gift of being His own children. They make this inquiry because they want to know God and to please Him. Also contained here is what God says to His children; how they obtain God's grace as they approach Him; the way to approach God; how a person can become a legitimate child of God; which of God's children He reproves. Finally, this step describes how she saw divine wisdom, which remained with her and enabled her to make true judgments.

The fourth step is the revelation of her own humble state, her transformation, and her divine reassurance. This step also contains how she saw the entire world and everything in it as something very small, but filled and overflowing with God; also, how in a state of rapture or ecstasy she saw God's power and will, a vision which answered every question she had about those who will be saved, as well as those already saved or damned, and about demons and everything else; she was content and satisfied with respect to all these matters. She does not know whether at that time she was in her body or outside of it.

The fifth step is the revelation of divine union and love. It begins with a wonderful revelation of the Lord's Passion, followed by an ecstasy of love. It then tells how she saw the Blessed Virgin interceding for the human race; also, how grace manifests itself in the sacrament of the altar. There is also a long teaching about the many ways in which the soul is made certain of God's presence when God has come to it, and likewise, how the soul knows when it has made God a welcome guest – which is something very different. It also includes a dialogue of the soul with the body (or sensuality), and a dispute between the soul and the body (or sensuality) after a contemplative experience. And finally this step mentions how there can be deception in spiritual persons, and also what the faithful and the unfaithful have in common.

The sixth step is the frequent and unbearable suffering and martyrdom, caused by the infirmities of her body as well as by the countless spiritual and physical torments horribly inflicted on her by many demons. This step occurs at the same time as the seventh step, which is more wonderful than all the others.

The seventh step is the revelation concerning which we can only say that it cannot be conceived (or, that it is not whatever can be conceived.). All of the previous steps – the revelations of divine intimacy, anointing, instruction, reassurance, union, and love – are nothing in comparison with this revelation. In fact, when I, brother scribe, asked Christ's faithful one whether what I put in the seventh step drew her soul more than the others, she answered that without comparison it was more attractive than all previous steps; she said, "It is so much greater that whatever I say seems either to say nothing or to speak badly of it." Then she said, "Whatever I say about it seems to me to be blasphemous; that is why I became so weak just now when you asked if it drew my soul more than the others so far, and I answered 'yes.'" Even so this most excellent step coincides with the sixth step for a time; then little by little, the sixth step vanished and the seventh remained.

The account which comes immediately after the introduction, although it belongs to the twentieth step, is nevertheless the first report that I, brother scribe, wrote of the divine words heard by Christ's faithful one. When I first began, I wrote somewhat carelessly and in summary fashion – as if I were writing a sort of "memorial"[31] for myself – and I wrote on a small sheet of paper because I thought that I would only have to write very little. But before long, after I had compelled her to speak to me, it was revealed to Christ's faithful one that I should use a large notebook for writing, rather than a single small sheet. But because I did not believe her, I continued to write on two or three blank pages, which I found in a

---

[31] The scribe's term "memorial," which has given the first part of Angela's book its title, appears here for the only time in the entire text.

little book of mine. Later, I needed to make a notebook of quality paper. And so, before I proceed any further, I think I should relate how I came to know of these things, and how I was completely compelled by God to write them down.[32]

The following account explains why I began to write: One time, while I was in residence at the friary in Assisi, Christ's faithful one came to the Church of Saint Francis; she was sitting at the entrance of the church and was screeching very loudly. Since I was her confessor, her relative, and her primary spiritual advisor, I was very ashamed especially because of the many other brothers who had come to see her there screeching and crying out; these brothers knew both me and her. There was also present that holy man, now deceased – the one mentioned above in the twentieth step – who wanted to give away all his possessions to the poor at the same time as she.[33] He had accompanied her on this journey, and was sitting in the church humbly on the floor not far from her, looking back at her and watching her with very great reverence and also a certain sadness. There were also other very good men and women, her companions, who were watching her and waiting reverently. But I was too embarrassed to approach her; my pride and embarrassment were so great that I waited indignantly at a distance for her to finish making those noises. And when she finished screeching, she got up from the entrance and approached me. I could hardly speak to her calmly. I told her she should never again dare come to Assisi, where such evil was possessing her; I also told her companions never to bring her there again.

Soon after this I returned from Assisi to our town, where she and I were both from.[34] And since I wanted to know the reason for her shouting, I began to compel her, in every way that I could, to tell me why she had screeched and shouted the way she had when she had come to Assisi. And after I assured her that I would never disclose these matters to anyone who might know her, she began to tell me a

---

[32] A narrative break, both in terms of technique and in terms of content, sharply divides the first set of twenty steps from the seven supplementary ones: while Angela tells the scribe the first twenty steps retrospectively and continuously, as past events dictated over a brief period of time, the supplementary steps are dictated as they happen, and this takes place in the course of four years, between 1292 and 1296, with numerous and long interruptions. These seven steps are longer and more elaborate than the preceding twenty.

[33] See note 27.

[34] This is the town of Foligno, in central Italy. The scribe keeps silent about it for perhaps the same reasons he never mentions Angela's name: he has promised not to reveal her name to anyone who might know her, as he states in the sentences below.

little about her story – which immediately follows this narration. I was astonished, and suspected that some evil spirit might be behind all this; I tried very hard to raise that same suspicion in her. Also I advised her and compelled her to tell me everything, because I wanted to write it all down, so that I could consult with some spiritually wise man, someone who would never know her. I said that I wanted to do this, so that she would not be deceived in any way by an evil spirit. And I tried to instill in her this fear by citing many examples of people who were deceived in this way – and so perhaps she likewise could have been deceived. And because she had not yet reached the step of very clear and complete certainty – a step which she later attained (as is found in the writing which follows) – she began to reveal her divine secrets to me, and I began to write them down.

As for these divine secrets, in reality, I could grasp and put into writing so little; I knew that I was like a sieve or sifter which keeps the very large grains but not the fine and precious ones. And I experienced at that time a special grace from God, which I had never known before, that enabled me to write very reverently and to fear adding any statement of my own, but only to write what I could grasp while she was speaking; I was unwilling to write anything after we parted company. But also, when I was sitting with her and writing, I would have her repeat many times for me what I should write. And in my haste, I sometimes wrote in the third person what she herself was saying in the first person; I have not yet corrected this.[35]

And here I can show that I was not able to grasp her divine words, except in a very superficial way. Sometimes, as I was writing accurately just what she was saying, I read back to her what I had written, so that she could tell me what else to write; she was amazed and said she did not recognize those words. One time, when I was rereading to her, so that she could check whether I had written well, her response was that my words were "dry and without any flavor;" this also amazed her. On another occasion she remarked: "These words remind me of what I said to you, but your writing is very obscure; the words which you read do not express clearly what they mean; that is why this writing is obscure." Also

---

[35] Once again the scribe interrupts his narration to self-consciously reflect on his task. His modesty is clearly more than a topos, and it refers to shortcomings of which today's reader must remain aware. He also explains the reasons for the switches he makes between first- and third-person narration: he never had the chance to go back and correct his text for consistency (he returns to this point at the very end of the book).

another time she said, "You have written nothing about the precious experience my soul is having; what you have written is inferior, and nothing by comparison."

And undoubtedly these defects were due to a defect in me – not because I added anything that she did not say, but because I truly was not able to grasp what she was saying. And she herself said that I was writing the truth, but in an abbreviated and diminished form. However, I myself think it was a miracle that I recorded these experiences in an orderly fashion, given that I was a slow writer, and that I then wrote very hastily, since the other brothers were gossiping because I was writing while sitting next to her in church. This will be made clear in the twenty-first step (or that of divine anointing), where God revealed to her and told her that I had written everything truly, although there were many defects.

Furthermore, if my conscience was confused when I went to write, the whole conversation between her and me was so disconnected that I could hardly write anything in order; therefore, as much as possible, I tried to go to her to speak and write when I had a clear conscience. Sometimes before our meeting, I would make a confession of my sins, because I realized that God's grace inspired me to ask certain questions, so that the result was orderly; it was divine grace, in which I could place my hope, that was wonderfully at work.

Even so, I continued to be very troubled and anxious, because I was omitting much that I knew was worth writing, due to my haste, and the inadequacies of my writing, as well as the opposition of my brothers, who gossiped so much that my guardian strictly forbade me to write, and the minister even reprimanded me. But they did not know what I was writing – and how good it was.

The First Supplementary Step

Here is the beginning of how and when I started to write, after Christ's faithful one screeched and cried out in the Church of Saint Francis, as was made known in the preceding account.

I, brother scribe, returned from Assisi to our home town, mine and that of Christ's faithful one. Using all my power and the authority by which I knew she was under obligation to me, I began to question her and to compel her to tell me the reason or cause of her screeching and crying out in the Church of Saint Francis. After such urging, and after my solemn promise not to reveal these things to anyone who might know her, she began to talk to me. She said that, when she was coming to Assisi, on that occasion about which I was asking, she had been praying throughout the trip. And among other things, she prayed for blessed Francis to ask God that she might experience Christ, and that blessed Francis might obtain from God the grace for her to observe faithfully the rule of blessed Francis, which she had recently promised to keep, and above all, that God would let her be truly poor and remain poor for the rest of her life.

She so desired to have perfect poverty that she went to Rome to ask blessed Peter to obtain for her from Christ the grace of true poverty, so that she might become truly poor.[36] And when I, after listening, read this account back to Christ's faithful one, she affirmed that it was true – though she said the writing had many defects; in addition, she said, "And when I approached Rome, I felt that I was given the grace of poverty that I had asked for."

And so, at that time, when she was going to the Church of Saint Francis, she kept asking him, blessed Francis, that is, to get this grace for her from the Lord Jesus Christ. And she mentioned many other thoughts that she had in her prayers during that journey. And when she came to the crossroads between Spello[37] and the ascent to Assisi, there, at the intersection of three roads, the following words were said to her, "You petitioned my servant Francis, but I did not want to send any messenger. I am the Holy Spirit; I have come to give you a consolation, which you have never tasted before; I will come with you, inside you, all the way to the Church of Saint Francis; no one else will notice. I want to speak with you continuously on this journey, and you will not be able to do anything but listen, because I have bound you to me, and I will not leave you until you come into the Church of Saint Francis for the second time; then I will withdraw this consolation, but I will never leave you, if you love me."[38]

And He began saying, "My daughter, my sweet daughter, my delight"; and He said, "Love me, because you are loved very much by me – much more than you could love me." And He kept saying,

---

[36] Angela's pilgrimage to Rome took place around 1290–1291.
[37] Spello is an Umbrian town not far from Assisi and Foligno. Very close to this intersection there still is a chapel dedicated to the Holy Trinity.
[38] It should be noted that Angela's first mystical encounter with God takes place through the sense of hearing rather than through vision; visions were more common among women mystics of her time.

"My daughter and my sweet bride."[39] And He said, "I love you more than any woman in the valley of Spoleto.[40] Now that I have settled and come to rest in you, just settle yourself in me and be at peace in me. You petitioned my servant Francis, who loved me very much and for whom in turn I did very much. And if anyone should love me more, I would do even more for that person. Indeed I myself will do for you what I did for my servant Francis – and more – if you love me."[41]

"And I began to have many doubts about these words, and my soul said to Him, 'If you were truly the Holy Spirit, you wouldn't say such things to me – it's not appropriate, for I am fragile and could become vain and boastful.' And He responded, 'Just consider whether you could become vain and boastful as a result of all that I've said: Try to escape from my words, if you can.' And I tried to want to become vain and boastful, in order to test whether He was the Holy Spirit, and whether what He said was true. I began to look at the vineyards around me in an effort to escape His words, but wherever I looked, He kept saying to me, 'That is one of my creatures.' And I felt an ineffable divine sweetness.

Then all my sins and vices were brought back to my memory, and I could see in myself nothing but sins and failings. And I felt more humble than ever before, but even so I was told that the Son of God and of the Blessed Virgin Mary had lowered Himself to speak to me.[42] And He said, 'If everyone in the whole world were now accompanying you, you would not be able to speak to them, for the whole world is already with you.' And to reassure me and free me from my doubt He said, 'I am the one who was crucified for you; for you I suffered hunger and thirst; for you I shed my blood – so much have I loved you.' And He told me about His entire Passion.

---

[39] This is the only reference to Angela as God's bride – an attribute widespread among medieval and later women mystics. It belongs to the topos of the mystical marriage, that intimate union with the divinity that was an essential component of medieval women's spirituality and which drew much of its imagery from the Song of Songs.

[40] This peculiar statement of preference on the part of the Holy Spirit is repeated, in similar though not identical terms, three times.
  Spoleto is another Umbrian town not far from Foligno.

[41] This sentence is connected with Angela's Franciscan spirituality, yet it is noteworthy that Angela, here as later on in this same chapter (as well as in the fifth supplementary step), places herself on a spiritual level that is higher than that of Saint Francis himself.

[42] Again, an auditory experience, this time of the second person of the Trinity. The meaning of the last part of Christ's statement is unclear.

And He said, 'Ask whatever grace you want for yourself and for your companions, and for whomever you please, and make yourself ready to receive it, because I am much more prepared to give than you are to receive.' At these words my soul cried out and I said, 'I don't want to ask for anything, because I am not worthy.' And then all my sins were brought back to my memory. And my soul said, 'If you were the Holy Spirit, you would not make so great an offer to me; if you were the Holy Spirit speaking to me, my joy should be so intense that my soul could not bear it.' And He responded, 'Nothing can be or come to be unless I will it, and so, for now, I am not giving you greater joy than this. I have spoken less directly to others – and one to whom I did speak directly fell to the ground senseless and sightless.[43] I am not giving you a stronger feeling, because I do not want your companions to know of my presence in you. But I will give you this sign: Try to speak with your companions and try to think either good or bad thoughts, and you will find that you will not be able to think about anything else but God. And furthermore, I am not doing all this because of your merits.' And then my sins and faults were brought back to my memory and I saw now more than ever that I was deserving of Hell. And He said, 'I do this out of my goodness, and I would not have done it, if you had come with different companions.' And these companions of mine were perplexed over my languor, since I continued to receive an intense sweetness with every word from Him. And I did not want to arrive, and I wished our journey would never end.

And I could not evaluate the intensity of the joy and sweetness from God which I was feeling – especially when He said, 'I am the Holy Spirit, and I am entering inside you.' All His other words gave me intense sweetness as well. And in my excitement I said, 'Now I will discern whether you are the Holy Spirit – if you accompany me just as you said you would.' Indeed, He had said, 'I will withdraw my consolation from you when you come to the Church of Saint Francis for the second time. But from now on I will never leave you, so long as you love me.' And He did accompany me to the Church of Saint Francis, as He said He would, and He did not leave me while I was in the church. He continued to be with me until, after eating, I entered the Church of Saint Francis a second time.

---

[43] This is most likely a reference to the conversion of Saint Paul, who was thrown to the ground and blinded by God while on the road to Damascus (Acts 9:4). Angela compares herself once again with one of the highest figures of Christianity.

And on that second occasion, when I genuflected at the entrance of the church, I saw Saint Francis depicted in the arms of Christ. And He said to me, 'I will hold you this closely, even closer than the eyes of the body can see. And now it is time to do what I told you I would do, my sweet daughter, my temple, my delight; for I told you that I would withdraw my consolation, but that I would never leave you, if you love me.'[44]

And as bitter as these words were, nevertheless, on that occasion, I experienced them as very sweet. Then I looked so as to see Him with the eyes of my body and of my mind . . ." I, brother scribe, at that point, asked her to tell my what she saw. She replied: "I saw something complete, an immense majesty, which I don't know how to put into words, but it seemed to me to be the All Good. And He spoke many sweet and gentle words to me as His consolation departed – and it was clear that He withdrew it very slowly and sweetly.

Then after that departure I began to screech and cry out in a loud voice; shamelessly I kept screeching and shouting, 'Love unknown, why do you leave me?' And I could not say anything else. I kept shouting without shame, 'Love unknown, why, why, why?!' However, these words were covered by my screams and were not expressed intelligibly. And He left me with a certainty that He was truly God. And I cried out wanting to die. And my pain was great because I remained alive. Then all my joints were dislocated.[45]

Later, as I was traveling home from Assisi, I was still filled with that very intense sweetness. On the way I kept speaking about God, and it was very difficult for me to keep quiet, but I tried as best I could to keep from talking, for the sake of my companions.

Also on the way back from the Church of Saint Francis, He told me the following, among other things: 'I give you this sign that I am the one who has spoken and is speaking to you: I am placing the cross and the love of God within you as a sign that will remain with you forever.' And immediately I felt that cross and love within my

44 Once more, Angela compares her experiences with Saint Francis's, finding her own to be higher than his. The stained-glass window described in this passage is found on the south side of the Upper Basilica of Saint Francis in Assisi. It portrays the saint being held by a gigantic Christ in his glory, accompanied by the Virgin Mary.
45 This is the first time that Angela mentions the dislocation of her joints, a strong example of the union of body and soul in her spiritual journey and of the bodily effects of God's presence.

soul; consequently, I could feel that cross within my body, and I could feel my soul melting in God's love.[46]

On the way to Assisi He had also told me, 'Your entire life: your eating, drinking, sleeping – every aspect of your life – is pleasing to me.'

After returning home, I felt a peaceful sweetness so intense – I don't know how to put it into words – and there was also in me a desire to die. To continue living for me was a great sorrow because of that peaceful, quiet, delightful, inexpressible sweetness. I wanted to go to that sweetness which I was feeling, so that I would never lose it – that is why I wanted to die and leave this world. Living then was more painful for me than the pain I felt at the deaths of my mother and children – more painful than anything I could imagine.[47] And I lay at home feeling this intense consolation, and in a state of languor for eight days. And my soul shouted out, 'Lord, have pity on me; don't allow me to stay in this world any longer.' On the way to Assisi He had talked about that delightful and unspeakable consolation in these words: 'After you return home, you will feel a sweetness different from any other you have ever experienced, and although I will not speak to you at that time, as I have spoken to you until now, you will feel that sweetness.' And I began to experience that sweetness or consolation which is ineffable and peaceful and quiet – I don't know how to put it into words. And I lay at home for eight days, and during that time I was barely able to get up to speak – even to say the 'Our Father.' He had told me on the way to Assisi, 'I was with my apostles many times, and they looked on me with their eyes, yet they did not feel what you feel; you do not see me, yet you feel me.'[48]

And I saw that this experience was coming to an end, and He departed very pleasurably while saying these words, 'My daughter, sweeter to me than I am to you.' And He called me, as He had before, and said, 'My temple, my delight.' And He did not want me to lie down as He left, so I stood up as He spoke to me, and He said, 'You have the ring of my love; you are engaged to me; you will never leave me. Let the blessing of the Father and of the Son and of the Holy Spirit come upon you and your companion.' He said this as He departed,

---

46 This passage underlines Angela's unique relationship to the Cross which, instead of being the object of a vision (as it was for many holy women of her time), becomes a part of Angela's bodily and spiritual substance – both in pain and in pleasure.

47 On this comparison, see the Introduction, p. 2.

48 Angela claims here that her experience of God is greater than that of the apostles themselves.

because I had asked for a special grace for my companion, and He said in response, 'I will give your companion a different grace.' And when He said, 'You will never leave me,' my soul cried out, 'O, I will not sin mortally!' But He replied, 'That is not what I am saying to you.'[49] After that I often smelled indescribable odors.[50] These experiences and others were such that I could not speak of them – I can hardly find words for them now – nor could I describe the sweetness and delight that I felt. And on many other occasions my conversations were such as I've described – but not so lengthy, profound, or sweet."

After she returned from Assisi, while she was lying in bed (as has already been mentioned), her companion, a virgin of wonderful simplicity and purity, heard a voice tell her three times, "The Holy Spirit is within L."[51] After that she went up to Angela and began to inquire: "Tell me what is going on with you, because I have been told what is going on three times." And Christ's faithful one responded, "If you have been told, I am glad." And she then confirmed what her companion was told. From then on, Christ's faithful one shared many of her divine secrets with her companion.

This same companion later told me, brother scribe, how on one occasion, Christ's faithful one was lying on her side in a state of ecstasy; her companion saw a kind of spherical star, as she called it, with a countless variety of splendid colors. And rays of remarkable beauty and varying widths shone forth from Angela's breast as she lay on her side; and the rays joined together as they shone upwards toward heaven. Angela's companion saw this with her bodily eyes while awake, at almost the third hour.[52] She said that the star was not very big.

Through a theological argument based on the integrity of the Trinity, Angela solves the scribe's doubt concerning who had in fact spoken to Angela on her way to Assisi – whether the Holy Spirit or Christ.

---

[49] God's response may be read as a rejection of the notion of quietism, or the impossibility to sin once a certain spiritual state is achieved – a notion embraced, for example, by the heretical sect of the Free Spirit, to whose doctrines Angela's are at times compared.

[50] Extraordinary olfactory perceptions are frequent among mystics. In addition to carrying a symbolic meaning, they also point to the involvement of all five senses in Angela's spiritual journey.

[51] Since the scribe has promised not to reveal Angela's name, he uses here the initial "L" to refer to Lella, a common nickname for Angela.

[52] The third hour corresponds to nine in the morning. As is often the case, Angela's companion reports and explains Angela's unusual behavior. In this passage, the physical effects of God's presence within Angela become outwardly visible.

She said to me: "One time I was thinking[53] about the great pain that Christ endured on the cross: I thought about those nails which I had heard pierced His hands and feet, and actually drove pieces of His flesh into the wood. And I desired to see at least that little bit of Christ's flesh which the nails had driven into the wood.[54] And then I felt such great pain for Christ's suffering, that I could no longer stand. I crouched to the ground, stretched out my arms and lay my head on them. And then Christ showed me His arms and throat.[55]

And then my earlier sadness turned into such great joy – I can't describe it; it was a joy different from other joys: I didn't see, hear, or feel anything else. It was so clear within my soul that I did not question it then, and I have no doubts now about what I saw, nor do I believe that I will ever lose that sign of joy in my soul. The beauty of His throat or neck was so great that I understood that it was due to His divinity; consequently, I seemed to see Christ's divinity through that beauty.[56] And I seemed to be standing before God, but I was not shown more than that. And I don't know how to compare that splendor to anything or any color in this world – except for the splendor which I sometimes see when the Body of Christ is elevated."[57]

The vision recedes and the scribe compels Angela to describe Christ's body further as she saw it in her vision.

And after being compelled to tell me what she sees in the Body of Christ, she began to speak, and she said: "Sometimes I see the Host – just as I saw His throat or neck – full of splendor and beauty which seems to come from God; and its splendor surpasses that of the sun.

---

[53] We can see here that Angela's ecstasy, rather than being brought about by the contemplation of a sacred image as was often the case for holy women who were her contemporaries, originates in meditation and intellectual prayer (although visions inspired by iconography are also present in Angela's journey).

[54] Christ's transfixion, which is not described in the Gospel, was the object of much devotional reflection in the Middle Ages, yet Angela's attention to the flesh driven into the wood by the nails – a detail that leads to a more general meditation on the Passion – seems to be unique among the mystical texts of her age.

[55] The physically submissive posture of Angela's prostrate body in the course of this vision accurately reflects the spiritual passivity that is intrinsic to the mystical path.

[56] The choice of Christ's throat as emblematic of divine beauty is bizarre or at least unlikely. It can best be understood as an element of Angela's peculiar use of language (what she later calls her "blasphemies"). Since God cannot be accurately talked about with normal words and images, then abnormal words and images are more likely to be effective.

[57] On Angela's Eucharistic piety, see the Interpretive essay, pp. 95–99.

Because of the Host's beauty, I am led to understand that without a doubt I am seeing God – although at home I saw even greater beauty in the vision of His throat or neck; such was the beauty of that vision of His throat that I don't believe I'll ever lose the joy it brought. And I don't know how to make this clear except by comparing it to the Host, the Body of Christ, because in the Host I see a beauty much greater than that of the sun. Still my soul is greatly troubled because I cannot clearly describe this vision."

She also said that sometimes she sees the Host in a different way, that is, she sees in it two very splendid eyes which are so big that only the perimeter of the Host remains visible. And she said: "Once the eyes were shown to me not in the Host, but while I was in my cell, and their beauty was so great and delightful that, as with the vision of Christ's throat, I don't believe I would ever lose the joy they brought. Although I don't know whether I was asleep or awake, I found myself in a state of very intense and ineffable joy, which I don't think I will ever lose."

On another occasion she said that she saw in the Host a vision of Christ as a young boy, but He seemed to be great and lordly, as one who has dominion. He seemed to be sitting and holding some sign of lordship – I don't know how to describe what He held in His hand. And I saw this vision in the Host with the eyes of my body (I always saw the other vision in the Host with my bodily eyes too). After seeing that, I didn't genuflect when the others did, and because of my delight and the depth of my contemplative state, I don't know for sure whether I then ran right up to the altar or whether I couldn't bring myself to move at all. I was also very upset because the priest laid the Host down on the altar too quickly. The beauty and the adornment of Christ was magnificent. He seemed to be approximately twelve years old. And the joy this vision brought was so great that I don't believe I will ever lose it. And my certainty was such that I have no doubts at all about what I saw. (And so it's not necessary for you to write it down.) And my delight was so intense that I didn't ask for help – I didn't say anything good or bad – I simply was delighted to see such priceless beauty."

The Second Supplementary Step

Christ's faithful one told me the following: "After that year (the one during which those divine statements were made to me when I was traveling to Assisi), while I was praying, I intended to say the 'Our Father' when suddenly a voice entered my soul saying, 'You are filled with God.' And right then I truly felt every part of my body filled with delight in God. And I wanted to die – just as before when I went to Assisi, and then returned and collapsed to the floor of my cell. This time too I collapsed. And my companion said that tears were streaming from my eyes which were open.[58] Then I was told, and I could feel, that God was embracing my soul; I felt that this was truly happening. But everything we say now seems like a joke, because my experience was so different from what can be said about it. And I am really ashamed to speak more accurately.

Also on that journey to the Church of Saint Francis, He had said to me, 'I will do great things in you in the sight of the nations; in you I will become known; in you my name will be praised by many nations.'

During those days, again while I was praying, suddenly the following very pleasant words were spoken to me: 'My daughter, much sweeter to me than I am to you, my temple, my delight, the heart of God almighty now lies over your heart.' Accompanying these words was a much greater feeling of God than I had ever before experienced. At these words, every part of my body felt delight, and I collapsed.

And He said, 'Almighty God has placed much love in you – more than in any other woman of this city.' "

God tells Angela that she will not receive a joy greater than what she can bear. She asks God for a tangible sign of divine presence but God gives her instead the love of God in her soul. God also anoints her with a secret oil that gives her great delight as well as the desire for a painful death. Then Angela has a vision of God in glory as Beauty and the All Good, and sees God's infinite love for her and for humanity. She is told that, in return for divine love, God only requires love. Angela understands God to be nothing but love. The scribe attributes to his need to hurry the omissions and abbreviations of his text.

As I, brother scribe, was writing, she said to me, "It would trouble my conscience to say what I am saying, if I had not been told that the more I say and continue to say about these experiences, the more they will remain with me."

---

[58] Holy tears and divine embraces are important themes of mystical literature. Tears are a grace that the mystic receives on the way to perfection, and they may indicate joy as well as suffering. The embrace is a prelude to the kiss of God, and thus an important step in the unitive stage of the mystic's journey.

And she said to me, brother scribe, "Yesterday and today I did not want to receive much. My conscience was troubled by what I said about the sign that I received and about the fact that I loved the tribulations, as you have written.[59] And today, while my conscience was wondering whether all that I've said about myself, and all that you wrote down was true, all of a sudden I received the following answer: 'All that has been written there is true; not one statement was falsely made, but the experiences were much more full or complete; and they were described inaccurately.' And He added that the scribe wrote incompletely and defectively. And He showed me that I had that sign. And He added, 'God is present in all that you are writing; He is there with you both.'"

Angela hears again and understands that God is present in what is being written. God appears as a doctor whose blood is used as medicine against the many infirmities or sins of Angela's body. She is forgiven, as was Mary Magdalen, and at this healing, as at the healing of every sinner, God as well as the sinner rejoice.

When I, brother scribe, finished writing the things just mentioned, Christ's faithful one spoke to me and said, "Now again I have been told something which has been so impressed on my heart that I can hardly keep from crying out and proclaiming it to everyone. It was made clear to me in the following words: 'No one will be able to make excuses concerning one's salvation, because people need to do no more than what a sick patient does before a doctor – show him the sickness and prepare to do what the doctor says. A person should do nothing more, and should not buy other medicines. One need only show oneself to the doctor and cooperate with all that the doctor says; one should avoid whatever contradicts the doctor's orders.' And my soul understood that the medicine was His blood; He Himself administers the medicine. The sick person need only rely on the doctor, who then cures the illness and restores health to the patient.[60]

In response to this my soul saw that every part of my body had its own illness. And my soul began to assign to each part the corresponding sin, which was seen and identified in a wonderful way. He

---

[59] The sign which Angela received from God earlier in this step and to which she refers here is a love for God so great that her soul will always burn for God. This is the sign which God gives Angela instead of what she herself had more modestly and tangibly asked for: a precious stone or a candle.

[60] The theme of Christ as doctor was widespread in both the patristic and the medieval tradition.

listened patiently to all of this, and then responded that He was very happy to immediately heal each illness in order. And He added, 'Mary Magdalen experienced that pain; for she was sick, and desired to be freed from her illness. Whoever has that desire can find health, just as she did.' "[61]

Angela is assured that her blessing of the alms is pleasing to God. Angela experiences great joy as the Virgin Mary speaks to her in church during the elevation and assures her that Christ loves her and is already present on the altar. Both the Virgin and Christ bless her, which causes great joy in Angela and prevents her from kneeling.

In talking to me, brother scribe, Christ's faithful one elaborated on the things mentioned above more fully, and with great power and clarity. That is why, when I read to her what I had written, she said that it was not complete, but rather, dry and abridged – although she did confirm that I had written the truth. She added that on the same day she was told: "After you finish saying what you have to say, be sure to add in writing that thanks should be given to God for all that you have written. And those who wish to remain in a state of grace should not raise the eyes of their souls from the cross – whether in joy or sorrow, which I myself may grant or allow."

She also told me while I was writing: "Once before a meal I was praying and asking Our Lady to obtain for me from her Son this special grace: that through the merits of His most holy Passion, He might take away all my sins, and absolve me and bless me, and that He would do this for my companion as well; and I also prayed that Christ, who blessed the meal that He shared with the apostles, would also bless what we were about to eat. Immediately after this prayer I received the following response: 'My daughter, my sweet, what you prayed for has been done: all your sins have been taken away, you have been absolved and you have my blessing (– I believe He spoke of my companion and me when He said 'you' –), and almighty God always blesses what you eat and drink while you live in this world.'

And I wondered whether all the alms that we receive are blessed when they are given, or only those that we eat. Immediately I received a response saying that all alms that we receive are blessed in themselves, so that they will benefit whomever we share them with

---

[61] In the medieval period, the figure of Mary Magdalen was interpreted in three, interrelated ways: as the converted sinner, as the contemplative soul, and as the woman involved in the Easter mystery.

in proportion to that person's disposition – such is the power of the one who blesses; even those who receive them in a state of mortal sin will benefit, because they will soon obtain a desire to convert and do penance.[62] And my soul perceived that God was within it, because of the spiritual joy and divine delight that my soul felt as truly coming from God."

She added that whenever she prays in this way before a meal, she always receives confirmation that she has been given all these gifts, and she perceives that God is delighted that she in her zeal still repeats this blessing.

During the elevation at Mass, the Virgin Mary tells Angela that Christ has already come into her. Angela is blessed by both the Virgin and Christ and experiences such joy that she is unable to kneel with the rest of the congregation.

And I, brother scribe, asked her whether on that occasion she had seen what she sometimes saw in the Body of Christ.[63] She said she did not, but she felt that Christ was truly in her soul. And I asked, "How do you know that it was really Christ?" She replied, "Because nothing so embraces my soul with the burning fire and pleasure of love as when Christ is in my soul. For on that occasion it was not the fire that sometimes burned in my soul; it was the fire of sweet love. And I myself do not doubt when such a fire is in my soul, because my soul knows that it is truly God, and that no one else can do this. And when this happens all the parts of my body feel disjointed, and I want it to be like this; all the parts of my body feel the greatest delight, and I wish I could always be in that state. And my body parts make a noise when they are disjointed. And I feel this dislocation more when the Body of Christ is elevated, at which point my hands are disjointed and opened.[64]

---

[62] Through these pronouncements, God seems to grant Angela (and her female companion) a kind of priestly power as intermediary between humanity and divinity, with food as the symbol which unites them. Furthermore, she obtains absolution without a priest. Such authority is of course unorthodox in the context of Catholic doctrine.

[63] Namely, in a vision occurring during the elevation of the Host at Mass.

[64] In this passage we find a clear example of the inseparability of body and spirit in Angela's mystical experience.

The Third Supplementary Step

Angela is told how God invites everyone to a banquet where God is both table and food; she also understands how the good is attained by way of suffering and deprivation, and that the special children of God eat from Christ's plate and drink from his cup. Angela understands God's love for humanity through a meditation on the suffering of Jesus, which the scribe claims he had to cut short due to haste. Because God descended into humanity, Angela is told that she must ascend into the life of grace. But suffering with Christ is necessary in order to be able to eat at God's own table. Christ's death is compared to the death of an innocent father who is put to death because of his children's offenses. The children will suffer the greatest distress when they pass by the place where their father died.

And so she was told: "Suffer and grieve, O soul, you who must pass by the cross on which Christ died. You should also settle down and rest there, because the cross is your refuge and your bed, and it should also be your delight, because there lies your salvation. One has to wonder how anyone can pass by the cross so quickly without even pausing." And she was told that if the soul were to remain fixed on the cross, it would always find blood there, freshly flowing. And with this example she was given to understand who were the legitimate children of God.[65]

After that, whenever I came close to a painting of the cross or the Passion, it seemed to me to be nothing in comparison with the extreme suffering which Christ truly endured, and which was shown to me and impressed on my heart. And so, I no longer wanted to look at such paintings, because they seemed to be almost nothing in comparison with the reality."

Through the example of her own joyful suffering, Angela answers the questioning scribe about the sweetness experienced by her soul when she is persecuted because of her love for Christ. When the scribe doubts that eating from Christ's plate and drinking from his cup

---

[65] The Latin word translated here as children is "filii," which can mean both children in general and sons in particular. Although the gender-neutral translation is preferable, still it should be noted that this expression also (though not exclusively) referred to the contrast within the Franciscan Order between Spirituals and Conventuals. For Angela, the legitimate children of God and of Saint Francis are the Spirituals, namely those who follow Francis's rule most literally and rigorously (for example, by observing complete poverty).

could be sweet as well as bitter, Angela again gives him a personal example.

"On Holy Thursday I said to my companion that we should try to find Christ.[66] Then I said, 'Let's go to the hospital; perhaps we will find Christ there among the poor, the suffering, and the afflicted.'[67] And so we brought all of our head veils, as many as we could carry, for we had nothing else. And we told Giliola, the servant at the hospital, to sell them and buy some food for the patients in the hospital. At first she kept refusing to do this, and said that we were bothering her; then, finally, since we kept insisting, she did what we requested: she sold our head veils and then bought some fish. And we also brought some loaves of bread which previously had been given to us to eat.

After giving this food to them, we washed the feet of the women and the hands of the men, one of whom was a leper whose hands were withered and decomposing. And then we drank from the water that we used for washing.[68] And the sweetness we felt was so great that it lasted all the way home – it felt as if we had received Holy Communion. In fact, because of that intense sweetness it seemed to me that I really had received communion. And when a scab from the leper's sores had become lodged in my throat, I tried to swallow it; and my conscience kept me from spitting it out – just as if I had received Holy Communion; and so I did dislodge it – not in order to spit it out, but so that it could go down my throat."

---

[66] Holy Thursday precedes Good Friday in the week leading up to Easter Sunday. It is customary on this day, also called Maundy Thursday, to reenact Jesus' washing of the apostles' feet on the day before his death.

[67] This is the hospital of Saint Felician, built in 1270 next to the Cathedral of Foligno.

[68] The figure of the leper is an important one in the hagiography of Saint Francis. The episode of Francis's kiss to the leper who turns out to be Jesus is one of the best-known among this saint's actions. The *Legenda Perusina*, to mention another encounter with a leper very similar to Angela's, tells that Francis reproached one of the brothers for bringing a leper inside the Porziuncola. But the saint quickly repented and forced himself to drink from the same dish as the leper – even though the latter's blood had flowed into it. Leprous blood and scabs are for Francis and Angela physical reminders of that suffering which lies at the heart of Christianity: the suffering of Jesus. Angela, like Francis, thus acts like the fool of God. This episode is discussed more at length both in the Introduction and in the Interpretive Essay.

Angela describes the condition and the destiny of bad Christians through two examples: a woman incapable of doing delicate work (likely, embroidery), and an indolent student. Angela is incapable of the sin of pride because of her awareness of being a vile creature.

She also told me, brother scribe, that on another occasion, she prayerfully asked God to teach her. And He first showed her how she had offended Him with every part of her, and He began with her hair. But I, brother scribe, could not write down this very beautiful, useful, and lengthy teaching, because we both had to leave the church, and later, because I was writing other things, I did not make the effort to record it.

Angela wonders whether it is better to know God in God's creatures or in one's own soul, but she does not give a clear answer. Similarly, she is told that it is not possible in this life to understand how, through transubstantiation, Christ's body is on every altar at once. Angela then discusses the importance of what is one's own and what belongs to others. During an ecstatic vision she sees divine wisdom as a dinner table about which it is presumptuous and illicit to inquire.

The Fourth Supplementary Step

God tells Angela to be of service to others and promises her that she will receive what she had asked of the Blessed Virgin: the certainty that she had not been deceived in the course of her mystical experience. God also allows Angela to see, say, and hear only what comes from God. When she does this, her heart is placed in God for three days and nights – during which time she cannot think of or see anything except God.

While in Assisi, she made as good a confession as she could so as to restore her soul, and prepare herself for receiving communion. And while Mass was being celebrated, she positioned herself between the iron grills in front of the cross. There the sweetest divine voice came to her and immediately restored her soul. It said, "My daughter, my sweet," and there were other very sweet words. But, even before this it seemed that God's divine voice had restored her soul; one of His statements was: "My daughter, my sweet, no creature can give you consolation – only I can."

"He later added, 'I want to show you something of my power.'

And immediately the eyes of my soul were opened, and I saw the single fullness of God in which I comprehended the whole world (that is, the land on both sides of the sea, the depths of the sea, the sea itself, everything). And in the entire world I discerned nothing but divine power – the experience is completely indescribable. Then my soul in a state of awe cried out, 'This world is pregnant with God!' And I comprehended the whole world (that is, the land on both sides of the sea, the depths of the sea, the sea itself, everything) as something small, but that the power of God fills and surpasses everything. And He said, 'I have just shown you something of my power.' And I realized that from then on I would be able to better understand other things.[69]

Then He said, 'Now take a look at my humility.' And I saw God's profound humility towards human beings, and my soul was in awe as it comprehended God's indescribable power and saw His profound humility. And my soul considered itself to be nothing at all, and saw in itself almost nothing but pride. And then I started to say that I did not want to receive communion, because I seemed to myself to be completely unworthy – and at that moment I was completely unworthy. And after showing me His power and humility, He said, 'My daughter, no creature is able to come to this point of seeing – where you have come – except by divine grace.'

And when it was nearly time for the elevation of the Body of Christ, He said, 'See, my divine power is now present above the altar. Indeed I am within you; and although you are receiving me, you have already received me. Receive communion with the blessing of the Father, Son, and Holy Spirit. I who am worthy make you worthy.'

And then an indescribable sweetness and intense joy settled within me, and I believe they will remain within me my entire life. And I have no doubt about this: I believe that I was given what I had asked for from the Mother of God which she had sought from her Son. I was satisfied that what the divine voice had promised me, had been fulfilled.'[70]

While Angela is sick and bedridden, God commands her to get up and kneel down in prayer. When, after great effort, she succeeds, she

---

[69] Another Franciscan as well as mystical trait is the contemplation of the world of Creation as a way of acceding, by means of analogy, to the knowledge of the divinity. On the metaphor of pregnancy, see the Interpretive Essay, pp. 85–88.

[70] At the beginning of this step, Angela had asked Christ's mother for certitude regarding the veracity of her mystical experiences.

feels joyful and healed. For four weeks, she is afflicted by spiritual aridity and by the memory of her sins.

"And during this time, the divine voice spoke to me saying: 'My daughter, you are loved by God almighty and by all the saints in paradise. God has placed His love in you. He loves you more than any woman in the valley of Spoleto.'[71] My soul doubted these words and cried out in response, 'How can I believe this when I am so full of tribulations? I seem to have been abandoned by God.' He said in response, 'When it seems to you that God has most abandoned you, that is when you are most loved by God, and He is in fact closest to you.'

Through Angela, God sends a message of humility to a friar.

And when it was time to eat, I prayed and asked God to take away all my sin, to absolve me through the merits of His most holy Passion, and to grant His blessing to me, my companion, and you."[72] She was then told, "You have been absolved from your sins, and I bless all of you with the flesh of that hand which was crucified on the cross." "Then I seemed to see that hand blessing us, and I understood that His blessing came upon the heads of all three of us. And I was delighted by the sight of that hand. And He said, 'The blessing of the Father, Son, and Holy Spirit be upon all of you forever.' "

Angela is given another sign of God's love.

"Following that exchange of words, on the same day, when I was about to wash some lettuce, a certain deceptive voice joined in and said: 'What?! Are you worthy to wash lettuce?!' And then, even though I clearly saw the deception, I responded with indignation but also with sadness, because this deception raised in me doubts about other statements that had been made. I said, 'I'm worthy to be sent to Hell immediately by God; I'm only worthy to gather manure.' "[73]

---

[71] This statement repeats what the Holy Spirit had already declared to Angela in the first supplementary step and, in different words, in the second supplementary step.

[72] The three people who receive this blessing are likely to be Angela, her scribe, and her companion.

Angela's sadness is reduced by hearing God saying that wine should be tempered with water. She once again desires confession and communion, but the friar does not come. God however consoles her and the following day she receives communion as well as the grace to give herself totally to Christ. She desires to suffer and die in martyrdom. Through the parable of a father who apportions his son's food, God explains why she is not given all that she desires.

And Christ's faithful one said this to me, brother scribe: "Ever since then God very often does wonderful things in my soul – things which I realize no creature could do – only God. For example, my soul all of a sudden is lifted up in God with such joy that, if it were to continue, I think my body would instantly lose all sensation and all use of its limbs. But God often plays this game in and with the soul: He withdraws the instant the soul desires to take hold of Him.[74] Even so, a very intense joy remains in the soul, together with such certainty so as to eliminate any doubt at all that this is truly God. And I don't know how to make a comparison with or even to give a name to what I see and feel. This experience is different from what used to happen to me – although this too is completely indescribable."

When she looks at the cross, Angela feels the presence of Christ in every part of her body. Christ embraces her with the very arms which were crucified, and she experiences great and abiding joy as well as the unshakable certainty that God is indeed at work within her.

"I rejoice in seeing that hand which He shows me with its nail marks, when He says, 'See what I have endured for all of you.' The joy which my soul experiences at this is indescribable. I can no longer feel any sadness about His Passion; instead with delight I rejoice in seeing this Man and being with Him. Now all my joy is in this suffering God-Man.

At times it seems that my soul joyfully and delightedly enters into

---

[74] The game between God and the soul is a common theme in mystical literature. It refers to the alternation between God's revelation and God's hiding (an erotic flirtation of sorts, if one reads it with the backdrop of the biblical Song of Songs).

Christ's side;[75] I can't at all put into words or describe this joy. That is why, when Christ's Passion was being reenacted in the Piazza Santa Maria,[76] at the moment when I should have wept, I, on the contrary, was miraculously enraptured by such great joy[77] that I collapsed to the floor and lay there speechless after this indescribable feeling of God began. And I tried to remove myself from the surrounding people, and considered it a miraculous grace that I could withdraw even a little. I lay there speechless, and without the use of my limbs. It was then that my soul seemed to enter Christ's side – and there was no sadness; in fact, my joy was so great that it can't be described."

Angela and her companion cry and long not to be deceived, though Angela is soon thereafter filled with certitude. Then Angela asks God about the Creation, the Fall, and the Redemption. In an ecstasy, God reveals to her that this mystery has neither beginning nor end, though she understands everything she had asked about and she understands about all God's creatures – the saved, the damned, the devils, and the saints. The vision has physical effects on her, as her body feels more agile, healthy, and invigorated than ever before. Her soul also feels quiet, stable, and peaceful. After this vision of God's power and will, Angela is lifted even higher where she sees God as the All Good, as indescribable as her joy.

The Fifth Supplementary Step

The revelation of the Lord's Passion as it appears here at the beginning of the fifth supplementary step, concerning divine union and

---

[75] While Angela's embraces with Christ were described thus far as external, this embrace takes place inside Christ's body. Nevertheless, body, mind, and spirit are inextricably intertwined. It is worth noting that Angela's devotion is directed at the wound on Christ's side rather than, as was to become more widespread later, the Sacred Heart of Jesus. The entrance into Christ's side was also a common theme of medieval women's mysticism.

[76] The Church of Santa Maria is located in Piazza San Domenico, the main square of Foligno. This is a precious historical reference because it constitutes the earliest record we have of the theatrical representation of the Passion of Christ.

[77] Angela's joy at the death of Christ, although it is not unorthodox because theologically related to a specific passage in the Gospel of John (19:19–22) – namely Christ's triumph over death – went nonetheless against medieval devotional practices, which demanded compassion at the death of Christ. Hence its transgressive originality.

love, was first recorded by a young boy in the vernacular.[78] I advised the young boy to write, since I, brother scribe, was prohibited by the brothers from speaking to Christ's faithful one, and so I myself was unable to write.[79] Consequently it was poorly written, and much was omitted – or so I was later told by Christ's faithful one after reading it to her; she told me to destroy it rather than leave it as it was. But because I, brother scribe, did not have the time to correct it with her, I translated it – just as I found it – into Latin, adding nothing (just as a painter does), because I did not understand it. And so, I found what follows written first in the vernacular.

Christ's faithful one spoke as follows: "Once I was meditating on the poverty of the Incarnate Son of God, and I saw His great poverty (at least as much as He showed my heart and wanted me to see); I also saw those for whom he had made himself poor. Then I felt and experienced such pain and remorse that my body almost gave out.

Then it was still God's will to show me more of His poverty: And I saw that He was poor in friends and relations, and I saw that He was poor in Himself – He was so poor that it seemed He could not help Himself. And although it is said that His divine power had been hidden by His humility, I say that it was not hidden – in fact, I received this teaching from God. Then I felt and experienced greater pain than before, because in this vision I recognized that my pride was so great that even afterwards I still could not experience joy."[80]

Angela sees Christ's Passion and questions His mother Mary so that she may know even more. Angela suffers greatly, and understands that her previous joy is gone. She then understands and shares even more of the suffering of Christ's soul. All joy is now gone. Her union with God however leads her to peace and contentment.

On Holy Saturday, following what was mentioned above, Christ's faithful one told me about some wonderful and joyful experiences of God. She told me, brother scribe, that on that same day, while in

---

78 The vernacular used by this young boy must have been the local Italian dialect spoken in Foligno.

79 In previous steps the scribe had already complained about the brothers' obstruction of his task, causing him to hurry because of their gossip and opposition to his encounters with Angela. Now he must resort to an intermediary – the young boy.

80 In this passage we clearly see Angela's thought seamlessly moving from spiritual meditation to theological understanding, from devotion to doctrine. This is characteristic of the *Memorial* and distinguishes it from the writings of other medieval women visionaries.

ecstasy, she was in the tomb with Christ. She said that she first kissed Christ's chest, and saw that He lay there with His eyes closed, as He did in death; she next kissed His mouth from which she received a wonderful and indescribably delightful odor breathing forth from His mouth. Then there was a brief pause. Next she placed her cheek on Christ's and He placed His hand on her other cheek and held her tightly; then Christ's faithful one heard these words: "Before I lay in this tomb, I held you this tightly." And although she understood that it was Christ who spoke these words, nevertheless she saw Him lying there with His eyes closed, and His lips motionless – as when He lay dead in the tomb. And her joy was extreme and indescribable.

One time, during Lent, as Christ's faithful one said, she seemed to be very dry; and she asked God to give Himself to her, because all goodness was dried up within her. Then the eyes of her soul were opened and she saw Love clearly coming towards her; she saw its beginning but not its end, for it continued; she did not know how to assign any kind of color to it. And immediately after it reached her, she seemed to see (more clearly with the eyes of her soul than was possible with her bodily eyes) that Love approached her like a sickle. One should not here understand a measurable or physical likeness – only that it moved like a sickle, since at first, Love drew back, not showing as much of itself as it had led her to understand it would, and as much as she did understand it would at that time; consequently, she became more languid. (Again, it is not a measurable or physical likeness, because it is an experience of her intellect caused by the indescribable workings of divine grace.) Immediately following this experience she was filled with Love and boundless contentment which, although satisfying, nevertheless produced a very intense hunger – so extreme that all her limbs became disjointed.[81]

The vision of the sickle leaves Angela languishing with the desire to feel and see God, so that she prays to God to release her from this life experienced as death. God speaks to her about love and hatred and gives her unshakable certitudes about her state of love. Between God's love and mortal love there is a third kind of love that is the source of joy. While in this state she can love reptiles, toads, snakes,

---

[81] This original description of divine love as a sickle can be interpreted through the mystical theme of the wound of love (immortalized by Gian Lorenzo Bernini in his famous statue of the ecstasy of Saint Teresa of Avila). The sickle is sudden and quick and sharp as a weapon, causing both pleasure and pain as well as an indescribable increase in appetite, love, and understanding.

and even devils; she could not suffer because of sin or because of the
Passion. While she naps, she experiences great delight at the ecstatic
vision of Mary and the crucified Christ – a vision that lasts three
days. While she takes communion, she is told that the All Good is
within her and she sees God as the All Good, who calls her by her
name and "my beloved."

And then she said that recently when she receives communion, the
Host lingers in her mouth; she said that it does not have the taste of
bread or of any meat we know of. "It most certainly has the taste of
meat, but of a meat that has a most flavorful taste – I don't know
what in this world to compare it to; it goes down sweetly in one
piece, not in little pieces, as it used to." She also mentioned how
quickly the Host dissolves and does not remain firm as before. "In
fact, it is so sweet as it goes down in one piece that, if I had not been
taught to swallow the Host quickly, I would gladly keep it in my
mouth for a long time; but then I remember that I should swallow it
quickly, and then that Body of Christ immediately goes down
together with that unknown taste of meat, and it goes down so completely that afterwards I don't have to drink any water.[82] This is not
what usually happens; usually, I have to make an effort to swallow
the Host, so that there is none left between my teeth. But now it goes
down immediately, and when it is down inside my body, it gives me
an extremely pleasant sensation, which, as can be observed, causes
me to tremble so violently, that I can drink from the chalice only with
a great effort."[83]

And while I, brother scribe, was writing down what she was
saying, as well as I could, while she was speaking, all of a sudden she
said, "Listen to what I was just told: God said, 'You have said much
to him, but you would not be able to say anything to him, unless I

---

[82] This is a reference to the medieval custom of drinking some water after taking
Communion.

[83] This passage is an important example of Angela's eucharistic piety: she experiences Christ's physical humanity in a bodily way and links the Eucharist with the
sweetness of God and with mystical ecstasy. Medieval liturgy and theology also
stressed the connection between the Eucharist and the five senses, even at times
to the point of seeing in the Eucharist the highest manifestation of the sense of
taste. Thus, although Angela's description of the taste of the Eucharist may seem
puzzling to today's reader, it fits quite well in the repertoire of Eucharistic piety
(including the taste of Christ's body in various forms) so widespread among
medieval women mystics.

will it.' And I tried not to tell you this, but there was no way I could keep from telling you what I was just told."

As I was speaking with her and writing she also said, "When you make the sign of the cross, does anything happen to you?" Then she said, "Something new has been happening to me recently: when I make the sign of the cross quickly and don't place my hand over my heart, I don't feel anything; but when I touch my forehead when I say, 'In the name of the Father,' and then touch my heart and say, 'and of the Son,' then immediately I feel a special love and consolation, and I seem to find the one I've named, there where I touch." And she added, "I would not have told you this, unless I had been advised to."

Angela feels the presence of God as a Pilgrim, and describes the ways in which the soul experiences this presence. She is reprimanded by other people and told to remain silent about this presence and its revelations because what she says is not found in the Scriptures.

"In addition to that feeling which assures the soul that God is truly within it, the soul is made to want God so perfectly, that the whole soul is truly in complete harmony with this desire for God. Similarly, the soul deceives itself when it says that it wants God without wanting Him in everything or in every way; this desire, then, in some way is not true; but when it is true, then all the parts of the body are in harmony with the soul, and the soul becomes so unified with the heart and with the whole body that it is one with them and responds as one for all of them. At this point the soul has a true desire for God, a desire which has been given to it through grace."

When invited to do so, Angela looks at God as an inexpressible spiritual reality. Another way in which the soul knows God is through an ineffable anointing that makes the union of body and soul totally harmonious.

"Another way in which the soul knows that God is within it is by an embrace which God gives the soul. Never has a mother embraced her child with such love, nor can any person from this world be imagined who could give such a loving embrace. God embraces the soul with a love that is unspeakably greater; He presses the soul to Himself so sweetly and so lovingly that I don't believe that anyone in the world could believe it, unless they had this experience." And when I, brother scribe, resisted her on this point about belief, Christ's faithful one responded, "Perhaps one could believe it, but not in the same way as one who experiences it."

"And God's embrace produces a fire which causes the whole soul to burn completely in Christ; it also produces a light so bright that the soul understands the fullness of God's goodness, which it observes in itself but which is truly much greater than the soul's experience of it; it is then that the soul is made sure and certain that Christ is within it. Still, all that we are saying about these things is nothing in comparison with the reality of the experience."

Then I, brother scribe, asked whether the soul experiences any tears in this state. And Christ's faithful one responded, "The soul experiences no tears, whether of joy or any other kind, because this is a higher state; when it experiences tears of joy, its state is much lower.

God also brings to the soul such superabundance of joy that the soul does not know how to ask for more; in fact, if it could remain here, it would possess a kind of paradise. And this joy produces effects and is evident in all the parts of the body; all bitterness or injury, or anything which confronts the soul in this state is made sweet. I could not conceal these effects from my companion."

Then I, brother scribe, asked her companion about this. She told me that once, while she and Angela were traveling together, Christ's faithful one's appearance became white, radiant, joyful and flushed, and her eyes became large and were so radiant that she did not seem at all to be herself.[84] And her companion said to me, "I was so sad and afraid that someone, man or woman, might pass by and see her. I said to her, 'It's no use covering your face. Your eyes are like candles burning bright.'" And this companion, because she was timid and very simple, and still did not know about the gifts of grace belonging to Christ's faithful one, began to lament and beat her breast, and she asked Christ's faithful one, "Tell me why is this happening to you? Try to hide yourself; we can't go around like this." She also said out of simplicity and ignorance, "Oh no, what are we going to do?" Christ's faithful one comforted and encouraged her by saying, "Don't be afraid. God will help us if we meet someone." This happened so many times that her companion said she could not count them.

---

[84] Angela's description by her companion conforms to one of the main physical side-effects of ecstasy, namely a lighting up of the mystic's face that eventually gives it a bright red color.

The joys of these ecstasies last for many days. It is impossible to recount the many ways that the soul knows of the presence of God as Pilgrim within it. God as a Pilgrim is ineffable, though what Angela knows about God is much greater than what the Scriptures reveal. God's coming into the soul brings unity between body and soul. In cooperating with the soul, the body finds great delights and sweetness. Spiritual persons can be deceived on the subject of love, for when love is truly pure (not mixed, that is, with self-interest or self-will) then spiritual persons consider themselves worthless, dead, nothing, and only then can their soul see the goodness of God and enter within Christ. Deception can also be experienced by spiritual persons in the process of attaining knowledge of themselves and of God's goodness. Angela then explains the meaning of poverty as the opposite of pride (which can only exist in those who possess something) and as the mother of all virtues.

The Sixth Supplementary Step

I, brother scribe, did not – indeed I could not – devote much time to recording the events from the sixth step (although I knew them to be useful and worth recording); this step contains the many ways in which she suffered: her bodily illnesses and the countless torments of body and soul, horribly inflicted on her by many demons. However, I did manage to write down some of the testimony which Christ's faithful one revealed: while she was speaking, I made a quick outline, because I could not understand her well enough to write a more complete account.[85]

Christ's faithful one told me that she did not believe her bodily illnesses could be described and the sufferings of her soul she said were even further beyond comparison. I heard her speak briefly about her

---

[85] At this point begins Angela's confrontation with darkness, her "dark night of the soul" (described most completely by Saint John of the Cross). The protagonists of this episode are God, perceived as impenetrable and hostile, numerous demonic forces that are further empowered by God's absence, and a suffering, desperate Angela. This suffering is different from the mystic's daily suffering. Rather, it constitutes an important phase in the mystic's itinerary into the divinity: in order to achieve mystical union with divine infinity, the finite soul must be radically transformed by God – certainly a painful transformation, because it has to overturn the human soul away from its lapsed state. Sanctification implies purification. This necessity must be kept in mind so as to avoid reading these lines as a meaningless descent into unspeakable horrors.

bodily sufferings; she said that there was not a part of her body which did not suffer horribly.

As for the torments of her soul, which she endured from demons, she knew of no other comparison for that experience than to someone hanging by the neck, with hands tied behind the back, eyes blindfolded, dangling from a rope – still alive, but without any help, without any support, without any remedy. She added that the demons tortured her even more cruelly than this, and that she suffered even more desperately.

The scribe reports how a trustworthy Friar Minor came to know and believe all that Angela says

Christ's faithful one said the following: "I see that demons are hanging my soul, and just as a person hanging has no support, so there seems to be no support left for my soul. All my soul's virtues are being subverted, while my soul looks on, knowingly, watching it happen. And when my soul sees that all its virtues are being subverted and driven away, and when it sees that it is powerless to oppose what is happening, its pain and anger become so desperate, that at times I am unable to cry, and at other times I cry inconsolably. And afterwards, sometimes I become so angry that I can hardly keep from tearing myself to pieces; at other times, the anger is so intense, I can't stop beating myself horribly until my head and other parts of my body become swollen. And when my soul begins to see all its virtues falling and withdrawing, I am overcome with fear and grief; and I cry out to God shouting to Him over and over again almost continuously: 'My son, my son, do not abandon me, my son!' "[86]

And Christ's faithful one said that each of her body parts was beaten and harmed by demons; and so, she believed that her bodily ailments – in addition to those of her soul – could not be described. She also said that demons revived all her vices; and although they did not live long, they caused great torment; even vices which were never hers entered her body, bringing great torment; these vices also were short-lived. She then said, "And when all these vices die again, I receive great consolation, because I see that I was handed over to many demons, and it was they who revived my former vices and added those others. And then when I remember that God was afflicted and despised and poor in this world, I wish that all my evils and afflictions would be doubled."

---

[86] On this invocation, see the Interpretive Essay, pp. 85–88.

Christ's faithful one also said, "While I am in that most horrible darkness of demons, where all hope of goodness seems to be completely lacking (indeed, that hopelessness is the terrible darkness), vices within my soul, which I know to be dead, are revived by demons from outside my soul; they also arouse vices which previously never existed in my soul.[87] And although the suffering is less intense in my body, there is such a fire in the three shameful parts that I used to apply a hot flame to them, in order to extinguish that other fire, until you prohibited me from doing this.[88] While I am in that darkness, I think that I would rather be roasted than suffer those torments; in fact, at those times, I shout and cry out for death by whatever means God will allow. And then I say to God that if He must send me to Hell, He should do it immediately, and not delay. And I say, 'Since you have abandoned me, finish me off and drown me.' And then I understand that demons are at work, and that those vices don't live in my soul, since it never consents to them – but they do act violently on my body. And my body's pain and weariness is so great that it would give itself up to death rather than suffer in this way. But my soul sees that it has been stripped of its power, and even though it does not yield to these vices, it is powerless to resist them; my soul sees that it is opposed to God, and it falls into them."

Angela is assailed by a new vice, so great as to be unmentionable, which she combats with a new and powerful virtue that God has granted her.

I, brother scribe, saw Christ's faithful one suffering more horribly in this sixth step than can be written down. This sixth step lasted for a short time, that is, almost two years, and it coincided with the seventh step – the most wonderful step of all – which began a short time before the sixth step. And I saw that this sixth step soon faded, without completely or totally ending – in fact, she continued to suffer many bodily infirmities especially. I also saw that Christ's faithful one remained in the seventh step, and continued to grow in God, more than can be described. And although she was always very sick

---

[87] The demonic darkness Angela describes in this passage is experienced as a martyrdom. Although it prepares her soul for the encounter with God, it should not be confused with Angela's later description of God as darkness.

[88] Through another allusion to self-torture as ascetic practice, Angela gives us a glimpse of a spirituality alien to modern mentalities. She refers specifically to the taming of her sexual impulses, although the text is somewhat ambiguous perhaps because of censorship in the history of the manuscript.

and could only eat very little, she was very plump and ruddy; still, all her body's limbs and joints were swollen and in great pain, and she could move herself to walk or to sit only very painfully. And yet, she herself considered all these bodily sufferings to be very light.[89]

Angela tells of the conflict within her soul between a certain type of humility (different from the one that brings her to the awareness of God's goodness) and a certain type of pride. This humility and this pride make Angela despair of ever being able to reach God.

These torments began sometime before the pontificate of Pope Celestine[90] and lasted for more than two years. "I was tormented frequently during this time. Even after this I was not completely freed from torment; sometimes now I feel some torment, although I experience it externally and not internally. And now that I am in a different state I know that there is an extraordinary purgation and purification of the soul in this struggle between humility and pride – because no one is saved without humility; also, the greater one's humility, the greater is the perfection of the soul. I also know that in this struggle between pride and humility, the soul is thoroughly burned and martyred, and so it recognizes the truth about humility; that is, through this humility it sees its true offenses and faults, which are punished, purged, and martyred by pride and by demons. Because of this, the more the soul is lowered, made poor, or humiliated, the more it is prepared, purged, and purified, so that it may be raised higher – because no soul can be raised up unless it is first lowered and made humble." The above account is a beautiful illustration of this.

The Seventh Supplementary Step

Christ's faithful one spoke as follows: "One time my soul was elevated, and I saw God in such brightness, beauty, and fullness – I had never seen God in such a way or in such fullness. And I did not see love there; I then lost that love which I had, and I was made not-love. After that, I saw God in a darkness – in a darkness because God is

---

89 The physical description of Angela's apparent good health in spite of her excessive fasting underscores her exceptionality (as well as the perceived "nutritional value" of the eucharist), while the description of her suffering reminds the reader of the physical effects of *imitatio Christi*.

90 The pontificate of Pope Celestine V lasted only five months, from July to December 1294.

a greater good than can be conceived or understood; in fact, nothing that can be conceived or understood touches or even approaches that goodness.[91] Then my soul was given a very certain faith, a secure and very firm hope, and a constant certainty about God, which has taken away all fear from me. And in this good which is seen in the darkness I was completely reconciled, and made so sure about God that I can never have doubts about Him or my possession of Him. And now my most firm hope, completely reconciled and secure, rests in this most effective good, which is seen in the darkness."

When the scribe questions Angela concerning the position of the saints in heaven, Angela experiences an ecstasy during which she sees the All Good and yet she sees nothing she can speak about. She sees the All Good accompanied by darkness, because it surpasses every good, and every good thus appears to be just darkness.

"When God is seen in this darkness, it does not bring a smile to one's face, nor does it bring about devotion, fervor, or fervent love, because neither the body nor the soul tremble or are moved, as they usually are. Rather, the soul sees nothing and it sees everything, the body sleeps, and speech is stifled.[92] And the many, indescribable displays of friendship, and all the words which God spoke to me, and also everything you have written, I understand that they are so inferior to that good which I see with such great darkness; consequently, I do not place my hope in them – indeed, my hope is not in them. In fact, if it were possible that all my previous experiences were not true, in no way would this diminish my hope, my most secure hope, which remains certain in the All-Good seen by me with such great darkness." And Christ's faithful one said to me, brother scribe, that her mind was elevated by this supremely wonderful grace only three times to that most high, and entirely ineffable way of seeing God with such great darkness. On

91 The last supplementary step begins with a radically negative statement about God as darkness – a darkness utterly devoid of sweetness, light, or love. This darkness is different, however, from the darkness experienced in the preceding step, for it now refers to the mystical encounter with God, to union rather than purification. The theme of divine darkness goes back to the writings of Pseudo-Dyonisius, so influential in the Middle Ages as to become veritable parameters for the interpretation of mystical experience. Central to Pseudo-Dyonisius is God's darkness and its inaccessibility to the human mind. Thus, the darkness of God is crucial to the theoretical writings of Saint Bonaventure as well as to the poetry of Jacopone of Todi – both Franciscans like Angela herself.

92 The language of paradox is essential to the mystical tradition, and is frequently used by Angela as well as other mystics.

many, indeed on innumerable other occasions, she had seen the All-Good, and it was always with darkness, but these visions were not as exalted, nor was the darkness as great.

Once when Christ's faithful one was sick, she said to me, brother scribe: "On the one hand, the world with its thorns repels me, because I consider everything in this world to be thorns and bitterness. Even demons repel me with frequent harassment and almost constant persecution, although they have power over me only because God has placed my body and soul in their hands; but no matter how much they may be able to harm my body, they cannot to the same degree torment or torture my soul, since the soul is more closed to them than the body. It seems I can almost see them in bodily form with their horns attacking me.

On the other hand, God draws me with Himself. But if I say He draws me with sweetness, or love, or with anything that can be named or conceived or imagined, that would be totally false, because He does not draw me with anything that even the world's wisest person might be able to name or conceive of. Even if I say that it is the All-Good that draws me, I destroy it. In fact, I seem to be standing or lying in the middle of the Trinity which I see with such great darkness. And it draws me more than anything that I have experienced so far, more than any good that I have ever talked about; it draws me so much more than these that there is no comparison; and whatever I say about it seems to be either meaningless, or abusive."

She then added, "It seems to me that I blaspheme. When you asked whether it draws me more than anything else so far, to respond as I did seems to me blasphemous. That is why I was so sick just now when you spoke and I responded in that way.

And when I am in that darkness, I do not remember anything about humanity or the God-Man, or anything that has form. Yet when I am in that darkness I see everything and I see nothing. And as I depart from what I have been talking about (or as I remain behind), I see the God-Man. He draws my soul with such gentleness, and sometimes He says, 'You are I and I am you.'[93] And I see those eyes and that face so pleasing and attractive as He embraces me. And that which comes out of those eyes and that face is the very thing I said that I see in the darkness, and which comes from within it; it is what delights

---

[93] It is significant that the highest mystical experience, namely the experience of unity with the divine (also known as "mystical marriage"), takes place for Angela not in the divine darkness but in the encounter with the God-Man, and it is expressed in nuptial terms.

me so much that it cannot be described. And while I am in this God-Man, my soul is alive; and I am in this God-Man much more than I am in God with that darkness. My soul is alive in this God-man, but God in that darkness draws my soul incomparably more than the God-Man. Still, I am in this God-Man almost continually – a condition which began when God gave me the certainty that there was no intermediary between me and Him. From that time on there has not been a single day or night when I have not continually experienced the joy of Christ's humanity.

I feel a desire to sing and give praise, and so I say:

> I praise you, beloved God,
> On your cross I make my bed,
> I found poverty a pillow for my head,
> Pain and contempt I found for resting
> In another part of my bed."[94]

And when I, brother scribe, asked her to give me a better explanation of what she was saying, Christ's faithful one added, "This cross is my bed because Christ was born, lived, and died in such a bed, and because God the Father loved this bed even before humans sinned. God loved the company of poverty, pain, and contempt so much that He gave it to His Son, whose will it was to lie on this bed in continual love and harmony with His Father. This is my bed, because I have been placed and made to rest here on the cross of Christ, who had a cross in His body, and a much greater one in His soul. On this bed I believe I die, and through this bed I believe I am saved. And it is impossible to describe the joy which I expect from those hands and feet, and from the nail marks which those hands and feet received on that bed. But I am about to say something, a song almost, to the Son of Holy Mary, 'What I feel I cannot speak, what I see I would never willingly depart from; for me to live is to die; therefore, draw me to You.' But as soon as I remembered about whom and to whom I was speaking, immediately I could no longer talk, my speech was stifled."

Angela's desire to die diminishes. She is frequently elevated into God, and her soul swims in these elevations. She understands that God gives differently according to divine criteria. Angela can best

---

[94] The image of the cross as bed present in this laud (a poetic form common to the popular piety of Angela's time) has obvious sexual overtones which connect Angela's mysticism to the bridal mysticism of her time.

know God through the understanding of divine judgments. The scribe admits that he cannot always understand all that Angela tells him.

And then Christ's faithful one said to me: "I heard God make the following statement to me: 'At the end of what you both are writing, be sure to add that thanks should be given to God for this writing, and that whoever wants to remain in a state of grace should not lift the eyes of the soul from the cross – whether in joy or in sadness, either of which I may give or allow to them.' "

When she is transported into God, Angela's soul understands so much more than it can on earth, yet this understanding is ineffable because it goes beyond human intelligence.

"And so when my soul recalls the Passion of Christ's soul, it cannot experience any joy at all, which is not the case when it recalls the Passion of His body; for then, after the sadness, my soul rediscovers joy. As I said, my soul understands the reasons for this; it also understands the acute pain in Christ's soul as He lay in His mother's body – the same pain He would later have, except He had not yet had the experience. As a result of all this my soul understands the judgments of God."[95]

Once while the conventual Mass was being said, Christ's faithful one heard God speak words to her, which are not here recorded. But when the priest who was celebrating Mass was about to receive communion, she heard God say to her: "There are many who break me and draw blood from my back." And she saw and understood that the Host, which the priest had just broken, was speaking to her. After thinking about this, Christ's faithful one prayed these words: "May he not be one of those." And God said in response, "He will never be one of those."[96]

Christ's faithful one said: "My soul was at that time full of joy, it was within the Trinity, and it was within the tabernacle where the Body of Christ is kept; and my soul understood that God was everywhere and filled everything, and it wondered why it took such delight in that tabernacle (for my soul was very much delighted and immensely pleased by it). My soul then said, 'Why do I delight so

---

[95] On this description, see the Interpretive Essay, pp. 86–88.
[96] On this paragraph, see the Introduction, p. 14. It is possible that the celebrant referred to here is the scribe himself.

much in this tabernacle? Why am I not everywhere so delighted, since you are everywhere, Lord?' And God responded to this with words so obscure that I do not fully remember them. But I remember He did say, 'By the words which I have the priest say, I am shut inside this little container; I do this by a special miracle.' "

On another occasion I, brother scribe, had given her communion. And because Christ's faithful one usually received some new grace with each communion, I asked her (as I had done many times) whether she was content with this communion. In response she said to me that if it were possible, she would want to receive communion every day.[97] She also said that a divine grace or consolation had been given to her at that communion, by which she understood and felt with certainty that communion purified, sanctified, comforted, and preserved the soul. She had felt and understood these four effects in her own soul at that communion more than she usually did. She also said that the divine voice had told her how communion benefits the soul in these four ways.

And on another occasion, at the elevation of the Body of Christ – I was the one celebrating Mass – she said that great joy came into her soul, and she was told, "This is the One who was crucified." And her soul saw Him. But immediately after she heard this, her soul was transported and was no longer fixed there; but a wonderful power was placed in her soul – the power of silence – a power which cannot be described. And her soul was immediately transported and wrapped itself in Christ's divinity. Then she was told, "This is the complete joy of angels, this is the complete joy of saints, this is your complete joy." Then after I reread this she said, "But truly this was said more pleasantly than what you now are saying; I barely recognize what you are saying."

Angela is told by God that those who practice the Scriptures should be commended more than those who comment on them. The scribe relates some practical difficulties in writing down Angela's visions. Angela recounts one of her daily visions of Saint Francis that took place while she was in Assisi for nine days. She then has a vision of God accompanied by a host of celestial beings.

Sometime after the preceding was written, Christ's faithful one said the following to me, brother scribe, as I was questioning her: "During the last Lent, I suddenly found myself totally immersed in

---

[97] In medieval times access to the Eucharist was infrequent for lay people.

God, more deeply than ever before. And I seemed to be in the middle of the Trinity more than ever before, for I received greater goods than before, and I was in those goods continually. While I was in God in this way, I was filled with joy and delights. And as I felt that I was in those extraordinary and indescribable goods and delights – which are beyond anything I have ever experienced – divine powers entered my soul, powers so ineffable that no saint or angel could describe or explain them. And I see and understand that no angel, indeed no creature, is large enough or capable of comprehending those divine powers and that most profound abyss. And everything I've just said speaks ill of and diminishes these things, so as to blaspheme against them.

And I was drawn away (and am now removed) from all that I had previously experienced and taken delight in: the life and humanity of Christ, and the meditation on that most profound company, which God the Father loved so much from all eternity, that He gave it to His own Son – I had taken such profound delight in these things: in the contempt, pain and poverty of the Son of God, and in the cross which was my resting place, my bed. And I was drawn away from that way of seeing God in that darkness which used to delight me. And I was drawn away from every earlier state so smoothly and sleepily, that I could not at all perceive it happening, but now I remember that I no longer have these things. For in that cross – which was my resting place and my bed, in which I used to take such delight – I now find nothing; in the poverty of the Son of God I find nothing; and in everything which can be named I find nothing."[98]

The soul feels God's presence in an ineffable way. God's disclosure is accompanied by increasing gifts, clarity, and certitude.

"In one way God makes Himself intimately present in my soul. And then I understand that He is present, and how He is present in every creature or in everything that has being: in a devil, in a good angel, in hell, in heaven, in adultery, in murder, and also in good deeds, and in everything that exists or has some mode of being, whether the thing is noble or base." And she said: "I understand that He is no less present

---

[98] The experience referred to at this point is described by Angela through negations alone (which is rather unusual for her), that is, we are only told what this experience is not: not Christ, not the Passion, not even divine darkness – though it shares with the latter several elements (such as its ultimate attainment of the Trinity and its inability to be conceptualized).

in a devil than in a good angel; and so, while I am in this truth, I take equal delight in God when I see or understand a devil or adultery, as when I see or understand a good angel or a good deed; in this way, God continually makes Himself present in my soul. And God's presence illuminates my soul with great truth and divine grace, so that, when my soul sees His presence, it cannot commit any offense, and it receives many divine gifts.[99] Then, since it understands that God is present, my soul is greatly humiliated and confused by its sins. Here my soul also receives very profound wisdom, divine consolation, and joy.

God makes Himself present in another, more special way, very different from the previous one; and He gives a different joy, because He gathers my entire being into Himself; He also operates many divine powers in my soul accompanied by much greater grace, and by an abyss so profound and indescribable that this presence of God, without any other gifts, is that goodness which the saints possess in eternal life. But as for gifts in heaven, some saints have more, others fewer. And although I can't speak of these gifts – since to do so would do more harm and blaspheme more than explain – I can nevertheless say that they are expansions of the soul by which the soul becomes more able to grasp and possess God.

And immediately after God has presented Himself to my soul, He opens and reveals Himself, expanding the soul and granting gifts and sweetness which are far more profound and beyond any prior experience. Then my soul is drawn away from all darkness and receives a greater knowledge of God than I could think possible; this knowledge brings such clarity and certainty, and is also accompanied by such a profound abyss that no heart could ever in any way understand it or even think of it. Even my own heart cannot go back in an attempt to understand it or even to think about it, unless God elevates my soul, because no heart by itself can ever extend itself that far. And so nothing at all can be said about it, because no word can be found to speak of or explain it; nor can any thinking or understanding reach these things, they are so far beyond everything; God cannot be grasped by any means. Indeed, God cannot be grasped completely by any means." Christ's faithful one affirmed with certainty and understanding that God cannot be grasped completely by any means.

---

[99] The achievement of a state in which it is impossible to sin is a defining trait of the heretical Sect of the Free Spirit. Although Angela is elsewhere vociferously opposed to this group, her theological speculations nevertheless come close to some of their tenets.

And she said: "Holy Scripture is so sublime that no one in the world – not even someone with knowledge and spirit – is wise enough to understand it so fully that one's intellect is not overwhelmed by it; even so one does babble something about it. But nothing at all can be said or babbled about those ineffable divine powers which God's manifestation produces in my soul. And because my soul is often elevated into divine secrets and sees God's secrets, I understand how Holy Scripture came to be, how it is both easy and difficult, how it seems to contradict itself, how some people do not benefit from it, how those who do not observe Scripture's teachings are damned and how it is fulfilled in them, and how others who do observe its teachings are saved; I see all this from above. And so when I return from seeing God's secrets, it is with confidence and detachment that I speak words about them; but these words are external to those ineffable divine powers which are produced in my soul, and come no where near to describing them. My speaking about them damages them; that is why I say that I blaspheme."

Angela says that there is absolutely nothing in this world or the next which she would trade for the visions she has of God as the totally unspeakable Good.

"And although at times I can experience small sorrows and joys externally, nevertheless there is a room within my soul where no entrance is made by any joy or sorrow, or even by the delight of any virtue or of anything that can be named.[100] But there in that room is the All-Good, which is not another good, or rather it is so completely good that there is no other good. And although I may blaspheme in speaking or in mis-speaking about this (since I cannot accurately put it into words), even so, I say that in this manifestation of God there is the complete Truth; in this manifestation of God I understand and possess the complete Truth which is in heaven and in hell and in the entire world, in every place and in every thing – I also understand every delight that is in heaven and in all creatures; and I understand all this with such truth and certainty, that I cannot possibly believe anything else in the entire world. Even if the entire world were to assert something else, I would scoff at this. I also see the One who is Being and I see how He is the Being of all creatures. And I see that

---

[100] The concept of a room (or chamber), not uncommon in mystical discourse, provides a useful metaphor for that part of the human soul where personal union with God is achieved.

He made me capable of understanding these things better than before, when I saw Him in that darkness which used to delight me so much. And I see myself alone with God, totally clean, totally sanctified, totally true, totally righteous, totally certain, totally celestial in Him. And when I am in this state, I do not remember anything else."

Angela understands how God comes into the Eucharist. She sees herself as full of sin yet continually in a state of quiet accompanied by a divine anointing. It is God who has placed her in this state which is above all others she has ever experienced.

She also related the following: "Once, during the feast of Saint Mary of Candlemas, when the blessed candles were being handed out for the celebration of the Presentation of the Son of God in the temple, and while that indescribable manifestation of God was taking place in my soul, just then my soul experienced its own presentation. My soul saw itself as so noble and sublime that I could never after think or imagine that my soul or even the souls of those in heaven could have or did have such nobility. And my soul could not then comprehend itself; consequently, if my soul, a thing created, finite, and limited, cannot comprehend itself, how much less could it comprehend God, the immeasurable and infinite Creator. Then my soul presented itself immediately to God with the greatest assurance, and without any fear; rather, I experienced more delight than ever before, and my joy was new and most excellent; I could never imagine another miracle in my soul so new and more clear. Such was my encounter with God. And when I had this encounter, I simultaneously experienced and understood that previous indescribable manifestation of God to my soul, as well as this new manifestation of my soul and its presentation to God; as a result, I experienced a delight different from all previous ones. Also the most sublime words were spoken to me, which I do not want to be written down.[101]

And later when my soul came back to itself, it found that it was pleased to endure all of its pain and injury for God; and that from now on no words or actions could ever separate it from God. And so my soul cried out and said: 'Lord, what is there which could ever separate me from You?' And I understood the response to be that there is nothing which could separate me from God. And I look

---

[101] This statement of secrecy on Angela's part is the other side of ineffability: there are aspects of Angela's experience which she does not *want* to disclose.

forward with great delight to the day of my death; the delight that day gives me, when I think about it, is beyond measure."[102]

After everything written above, Christ's faithful one told me, brother scribe, that she heard God tell her – in words more wonderful than she could relate – that this indescribable good mentioned above is what the saints possess in eternal life. The good possessed by the saints in eternal life is no different from that good mentioned above; but there is a different experience of it there. In fact the experience of this good in eternal life is so different and varied in comparison with the experience recorded here, that a minor saint, who possesses less of the good in eternal life, has more than can be given to any soul in this life before the death of the body. She said that her soul understood this. – Thanks be to God always. Amen.

God tells Angela that the faithful, meaning the saints, are wherever God is, and that Angela also is everywhere God is found.

Epilogue

I, brother scribe, after I had written almost all that this little book contains, asked Christ's faithful one to ask and request of God that, if I had written anything false or superfluous here, God would in His mercy reveal it and show it to her, so that we would know the truth about these things from God Himself. And Christ's faithful one responded to me by saying: "I have already asked God many times to let me know whether I have spoken or you have written a superfluous or false word, so that I could at least make a confession of it. God's response to me was that everything that I said and that you wrote was entirely true, and that there was nothing false or superfluous." She also said: "I have spoken temperately to you; for God had said many other things to me which I could have told you to write, but which I did not mention." She also said that God Himself told her the following: "Everything which has been written, all of it, was written in accordance with my will, and has come from me, that is, it proceeded from me." Then God said: "I will seal this work." "And since I did

---

[102] This final passage deals with the theme of self-knowledge (traditionally, a moral, metaphysical, and theological question, although today we see it as psychological). Angela approaches it from a mystical perspective, concluding her *Memorial* both with a note of reticence (an allusion to 2 Corinthians 12:4) and with her own suspension between infinity and nothingness, between her God and her Self.

not understand what was meant by 'I will seal this,' God said, 'I will put my signature on this.' "

I, brother scribe, have written this with great fear and reverence, and I have written very hastily the words of Christ's faithful one while she was speaking in my presence. And I did not add anything of my own, from the beginning to the end, but I did omit many good things which she said, because I could not understand them, nor could I write them down.

She spoke about herself using the first person; but sometimes in my haste I recorded what she said in the third person; I have not corrected this. And from the beginning to the end I hardly wrote anything unless she was speaking to me in person. Then I would write her words as she uttered them – in great haste, since many impediments and prohibitions from my brothers forced me to work rapidly.

And I also tried to use her own words – the ones I could grasp – since I did not want to write – nor did I know what to write – when she was not present, out of fear and zeal, so that I would not use even one word which she had not really spoken. That is why I always reread to her what I had written, repeating it many times, so that I would use only her very own words.

Furthermore, the Lord saw to it that two other truly faithful friars, who were familiar with Christ's faithful one, saw these writings and heard her speak; they also examined and discussed these things with her many times.[103] And what is more, these friars were made certain of this work's validity by the Lord's divine grace, and they bear faithful witness to it both in word and in deed.

---

[103] The names of these friars are unknown.

Interpretive Essay

The Spirit and the Flesh in Angela of Foligno

Does the *Memorial* have anything to say that is significant for today's reader? Does Angela of Foligno's quest bear any connection with our own; do her dilemmas concern the issues that tear us apart; is her joy continuous with ours? Or has her experience become by now so peculiar and anachronistic, so intolerably remote from our own as to be of interest to the medieval scholar alone? And is Angela's mysticism, like that of other holy women who were her contemporaries, disruptive to the patriarchal order in which it was embedded, or does it instead collude with it by acting out its misogyny? One fundamental question informs the relationship between women and Christianity, and it has been eloquently formulated by the noted theologian Elisabeth Schüssler-Fiorenza: "Is being a woman and being a Christian a primary contradiction that must be resolved in favor of one to the exclusion of the other? Or can both be kept in creative tension so that my being a Christian supports my struggle for liberation as a woman, and my being a feminist enhances and deepens my commitment to live as a Christian?"[1] A complex spectrum of answers can be imagined, ranging from total rejection of Christianity to orthodox commitment to its precepts. Likewise, numerous questions arise when the contemporary reader is faced with a medieval text such as Angela of Foligno's *Memorial*.

Certainly our age is profoundly different from Angela of Foligno's, yet it is also important to recognize to what extent the questions this mystic asks of herself and of God resemble many that are still raised today. More specifically, it is possible and useful to relate a reading of Angela of Foligno's *Memorial* to some of the issues that are central to the undertaking of contemporary Christian feminist theology. For Angela's focus on the role of the spirit and that of the body and the relation between these two aspects of the self, as well as her intense concern with and meditation on the use of language, place her intellectual and spiritual pursuits in an uncanny continuity with the work of many contemporary feminists and theologians. Furthermore, Angela

---

[1]   Elisabeth Schüssler-Fiorenza, *Bread Not Stone: The Challenge of Feminist Biblical Interpretation* (Boston: Beacon Press, 1984), 53.

is an important character in that history of women that, for obvious reasons, needs to be uncovered and recovered. As Grace Jantzen has rightly noted, by silencing the voices of mystics "a whole tradition of challenge to the values of power and competition, the hallmarks of patriarchy, has been made unavailable to women."[2]

It is precisely the more or less explicit presence of gender – of women's self-awareness as females both biologically and culturally – at the heart of the reflection undertaken by both Angela and feminist theology which can effectively mediate between a medieval and a contemporary approach to the issues of spirit, body, and language. This should not be surprising, given the fact that the mystical way has been one of the few possibilities women had, in the Middle Ages and later, to achieve a certain stature in both lay and religious society. As Eleanor McLaughlin puts it, medieval Christian women "through this ideal of sanctity moved beyond the limitations of biology and social convention, especially as these touched their womanhood, to an uncommon integration of act and vision, reason and love, obedience and self-affirmation."[3] If traditional scholarship on mysticism has focused on things spiritual, thus reinforcing a dualism between flesh and spirit that is antithetical to Angela's embodied spirituality, much contemporary scholarship has instead shifted its critical attention to the role of the body in the spiritual investigations described by mystical discourse. A reflection on the body as it relates to spirit and to language is indeed the most important point of contact between Angela of Foligno and contemporary feminist theology. Topics such as eroticism, maternity, food, the Incarnation, and physical suffering regularly punctuate both the *Memorial* and recent theological treatises as issues that have hardly been resolved in the centuries that have intervened between Angela's age and our own. And if terms such as transgression, abjection, *écriture féminine*, and *jouissance* may sound all-too modern (whether exquisitely or uncomfortably so), still the issues these terms describe have a central role in Angela's text as well. Such topics are indeed closely linked to theological and devotional questions such as transubstantiation, or the transformation of the Host into the body and blood of Christ at the moment of the consecration, and *imitatio Christi*, namely the project of imitating Christ's suffering – across the borders of mind, flesh, and spirit – undertaken by so many Christian mystics.

---

2 Grace Jantzen, *Power, Gender, and Christian Mysticism* (Cambridge: Cambridge University Press, 1995), 11.

3 Ann Loades, ed., *Feminist Theology: A Reader* (London: SPCK, 1990), 116.

Feminist theology takes as one of its points of departure the fundamental ambivalence toward women that characterizes the Christian
tradition. If it is obvious to most that Christ's redemption is directed
to both women and men, that the term "God" does not refer to a
bearded old man, and that women are as valuable as men both in the
order of Creation and in the Beyond, what is even more obvious to
many is the misogyny of many fundamental Christian authors, and
the male-centered, woman-erasing traditional readings of Christian
Scriptures. So, for example, Christian discourse has insisted on
woman's derivation from man (by stressing the Genesis story
whereby Eve was fashioned out of Adam's rib), and especially on her
passivity and association with the flesh rather than with the mind or
even the spirit. Hence the need for feminist theology and, more
generally, for a renewed understanding of the position of women
within the Christian faith and its historical tradition.

Angela does not and indeed could not argue in these modern terms,
of course, yet the *Memorial* shows that she is surely self-conscious of
herself as a woman, as a gendered being. Her gender plays an important role in her spiritual quest as well as in her worldly experiences.
From a practical viewpoint, for example, Angela fears begging – an
activity that becomes necessary for her survival, given her Franciscan embrace of complete poverty – because she is an attractive and
still rather young woman: "since I was young, begging could be
dangerous as well as shameful for me" (28).[4] In a more positive light,
God's love for Angela is the love for a woman, as she openly, even
brazenly insists no less than three times. On separate occasions, God
tells her: "I love you more than any woman in the valley of Spoleto"
(41); "Almighty God has placed much love in you – more than in any
other woman of this city" (48); "God . . . loves you more than any
woman in the valley of Spoleto" (56). From a more negative perspective, God's criticism of Angela is aimed at one of her feminine
features – her hairstyle: "He first showed her how she had offended
Him with every part of her and He began with her hair" (54). More
generally and meaningfully, Angela's past experiences as wife and
mother thoroughly inform her visions of God, as I will develop
further later in this essay. Even the topos of woman's passivity, rather
than negatively signifying lack of importance, is elevated to perfection within mystical discourse in general and Angela's in particular;
for her continuous linguistic use of the passive voice accurately

---

4   All page numbers refer to John Cirignano's translation in this book.

reflects the spiritual passivity necessary, regardless of one's gender, in order to be assumed within the Trinity. Angela's spiritual journey is punctuated by a conspicuous degree of transgression that paradoxically stems from her will to obey. She derives her spiritual strength precisely from strict obedience to God, whose will and desire she follows at all costs. This type of obedience, which is the very opposite of the passive submission the word might evoke for us today, then impels Angela to break every rule and disregard every statement that does not conform exactly to what God explicitly tells her in the course of their numerous encounters. At the linguistic level this contrast between world and vision results in what Angela herself repeatedly describes as blasphemies, to which I return later in this essay. In terms of behavior, it leads for example to scandalous screeching fits that embarrass all those around her – first and foremost her confessor and scribe, who forbids her from ever returning to the Basilica of Saint Francis in Assisi (where she had her first important screeching episode as the vision of a loving God departed from her). As Angela herself puts it, "if I heard any talk of God, I would start screeching. Even if someone had stood over me with an axe to kill me, I would not have been able to keep from screeching" (32).

It is not only her screeching that cannot be stopped (and is thus reminiscent of the English mystic's Margery Kempe's uncontrollable tears and sobs). Toward the beginning of the *Memorial*, when she tells of her strong desire to give away all her possessions, Angela states quite unequivocally that, in spite of tempting and assaulting demons, all the friars who counseled her, and her own confessor, she "could not possibly ignore" this desire, "no matter what good or bad things might happen to me" (29). The virtue of obedience, especially extolled among the laity in the case of women, is used by Angela in an ingenious way that paradoxically allows, even mandates her to transgress: obedience to God demands the constant infraction of human rules. The radical choice made by Angela contradicts the laws of common sense. And she does give up absolutely everything she owns in order to serve the needy in prayer and in action. Visions of the divine give Angela the inspiration and the power to resist patriarchal pressures to conform to woman's silent image, so that her spiritual itinerary is inextricably bound up with her worldly journey.

It should by now be quite clear that Angela's story diverges from the stereotype of the medieval pious woman, a virgin who spends her life praying within the walls of a convent, shielded from the outside world. (Though virginity had its advantages, as André Vauchez so well explains: "not wanting to be just an object or a body, woman finds in religious life – whether or not cloistered – which legitimates and sacralizes virginity, a freedom and an autonomy that lay society refused her.")[5] Before dictating the *Memorial*, Angela had been married, borne children, and sinned, and she continued throughout her life to live in this world her double vocation of prayer and service, meditation and action. Her otherworldliness, her world-denying spirituality, to refer to an important essay by Beverly Wildung Harrison, does not entail the reactionary escapism of the privileged, but rather it "encourages an ongoing struggle against the present order by conjuring a better time and a better place, beyond the oppressive here and now."[6] The holiness Angela pursues denies the value of this world in favor of life with and in God, yet an important consequence of this choice is not the negation of the body but rather its exaltation, even in suffering, as a vehicle to God. Through her holiness, her visions and strict obedience to them, through her desire of God (hers for God, God's for her), Angela of Foligno attains the power of authority on this earth – to speak, to dictate, to be listened to and followed in spite of her lack of the formal education that would make her officially qualified to do so – as well as union with the divinity: a temporary union on this earth, an eternal union in the afterlife.

But like many women today, Angela must have intensely experienced the conflicts between spiritual demands and the many demands of her family. Her transgression of family values is most obvious in her notorious prayer to God that her family – mother, husband, children – should die. However scandalous to the modern reader, this request illustrates painfully (for Angela does experience pain at the death of at least her mother and children, as she states later in the *Memorial*) both the Christian tradition of distrust toward family as obstacle to spiritual perfection and today's concern, especially alive among women, on how to satisfactorily reconcile personal and familial needs, the growth of self and the nurturing of those closest to us (who may, like children, physically need us in order to fill their most basic needs). In this perspective, Angela's prayer takes on a poignant dimension. For if we set aside the self-righteous

5 André Vauchez, "L'idéal de sainteté dans le mouvement féminin franciscain aux XIIIe et XIVe siècles," in *Movimento religioso femminile e francescanesimo nel secolo XIII* Atti del VII Convegno Internazionale, Assisi, 11–13 ottobre 1979 (Assisi: Società Editrice di Studi Francescani, 1980): 315–337, 332. My translation.
6 Loades, 198.

indignation this particular prayer of hers is likely to elicit at first sight, we may read in it instead the despair of a woman who must pray for the destruction of those she loves most in order to be allowed to do what she cannot, in any case, stop herself from doing: follow God, find herself, help others, save her soul.

That women mystics derived power from a lifestyle that seems to us the epitome of powerlessness is a common theme among feminist critics of medieval mysticism. The best-known of these is probably Caroline Walker-Bynum, who states in her brilliant book *Holy Feast and Holy Fast* that "the extreme asceticism and literalism of women's spirituality were not, at the deepest level, masochism or dualism but, rather, efforts to gain power and to give meaning."[7] In a fascinating essay, Eleanor McLaughlin states most unequivocally that "the spirituality of the women who were called holy by their friends, their neighbours and the Church was a source of wholeness, meaning, power, and authority. The effectiveness of these women was rooted in their holiness. Power out of holiness."[8] Laurie Finke, from a sophisticated and persuasive perspective of cultural studies influenced by the work of French philosopher Michel Foucault, claims that "mystics took disciplines designed to regulate and subject the body and turned them into . . . methods of consolidating spiritual power and authority."[9] And Grace Jantzen devotes an important book, significantly entitled *Power, Gender, and Christian Mysticism*, to unraveling her convincing thesis that "what mysticism is and who counts as a mystic . . . will always reveal interconnected struggles of power and gender," namely, as she concludes, that "who counts as a mystic rests just as much on issues of power and gender as it does on an individual's experiences and beliefs."[10]

How do Angela's experiences as a woman shape her spiritual itinerary and the *Memorial*, the text which recounts it? Embodiment, central to the undertakings of both Angela of Foligno and feminist theologians, is the category that describes the many ways in which gender plays an active textual role in the *Memorial*. This entails the

[7] Caroline Walker Bynum, *Holy Feast and Holy Fast: The Religious Significance of Food to Medieval Women* (Berkeley: University of California Press, 1987), 208.

[8] Loades, 100.

[9] "Mystical Bodies and the Dialogics of Vision," in *Maps of Flesh and Light: The Religious Experience of Medieval Women Mystics*, ed. Ulrike Wiethaus (Syracuse, NY: Syracuse University Press, 1993): 28–44, 94.

[10] Grace Jantzen, *Power, Gender, and Christian Mysticism* (Cambridge: Cambridge University Press, 1992), 2, 264.

active participation in spirituality not only of the body but also of the numerous activities connected with the fact that we humans are indeed embodied beings. Many of these activities, specifically the ones that involve caring for the body (one's own as well as those of one's family members), have been traditionally associated with women's role as carers and carriers. The most obvious examples of this include bearing, giving birth to, and nurturing children, preparing the family meals, taking care of the sick, the elderly, the dying, preparing the dead for burial. These situations provide female contexts, images, and metaphors for the woman mystic's union with God and for her spiritual journey in general.

In the *Memorial*, an unforgettable episode of this sort takes place as Angela is immersed in a most prosaic domestic activity when some demons attempt, in vain, to fool her: " 'What?! Are you worthy to wash lettuce?!' " (56). Thanks to her intimacy with God and her knowledge of God's language, Angela understands immediately that the message does not come from God, and retorts ingeniously in her characteristic way: " 'I'm worthy to be sent to Hell immediately by God; I'm only worthy to gather manure' " (56). That must have shut the demons up. But be it the unwanted company of demons or the desirable presence of God, the point is that washing lettuce, preparing food – a daily task for most women then and now – is not incompatible with spiritual encounters, on the contrary. In the words of Nicola Slee, "to discover the presence of God within the confines of the mundane and domestic is radically and explosively to transform these realities – and this may be as uncomfortable as it is unexpected."[11] To find dirty lettuce in the midst of a mystical treatise is certainly unexpected. And reading about it can transform our understanding of everyday tasks. It is God who tells Angela, while she is travelling on the road to Assisi, "Your entire life: your eating, drinking, sleeping – every aspect of your life – is pleasing to me." (44). God's own words convert for Angela the quotidian into the miraculous.

The awe-inspiring yet very physical act of giving birth, for example, is often described as being miraculous even in today's secularized worldview. It is not at all surprising that this should be the view of a Christian perspective. As Janet Morley has noted, "Many women have found the experience of pregnancy, breastfeeding and nurturing children to be powerful images of the all-embracing tenderness of God towards us."[12] Several important

---

[11] Loades, 42.
[12] Loades, 160.

images in the *Memorial* are derived from the realm of maternity, of which Angela had bodily as well as spiritual knowledge. In order to describe the active presence of God in the creation, Angela reverses a traditional image and exclaims: " 'This world is pregnant with God!' And I comprehended the whole world (that is, the land on both sides of the sea, the depths of the sea, the sea itself, everything) as something small, but that the power of God fills and surpasses everything' " (55). God the creator of the world is paradoxically seen as contained (though not successfully) by the creation as a child by the mother's womb – rather than as a masculine progenitor instilling life into his offspring. It is this vision of God as child within the womb of creation that gives Angela an increased knowledge of what surrounds her: "I realized that from then on I would be able to better understand other things" (55). The interchange between creator and creation returns later in the *Memorial* in a striking reversal of Christ's call of abandonment on the Cross: "I cry out to God shouting to Him over and over again almost continuously: 'My son, my son, do not abandon me, my son!' "(65).

Not only does Angela make use of an image of maternity, but she even goes so far as to posit herself both as God's mother (she calls for Christ as her son) and as Christ himself on the Cross, crying out on the brink of despair (an instance of her *imitatio Christi*, to which I return below). These intersecting images, new and bold, underline the difference between spiritual humility and worldly modesty: Angela is humble for she sees her finiteness and inherent sinfulness, but she certainly does not strike the reader as modest in the human sense. Her complex images focus on maternity as well as on that relationality and connectedness that is the essence of maternity, without which maternity could not exist. For God is not the isolated and unrelated "wholly other" for Angela. Rather, God is portrayed in images of exchange and mutuality, of relationships such as (though not only) the filial and the maternal. These images support the feminist critique that "where our image of transcendence is represented to us as unrelatedness, as freedom from reciprocity and mutuality, the experience of God as living presence grows cold and unreal."[13] Angela's burning spirituality makes such traditional imagery impossible: the God she describes is open to human contact and is vulnerable to others – as the Passion demonstrates. Thus, with another image drawn from her experience of maternity, Angela understands "the acute pain in Christ's soul as He lay in His mother's body" (71).

13 Loades, 209.

Once again, Angela's double identification is both with Christ and with Christ's mother, with a divine spirit and a human flesh that cannot be separated from each other.

In the depictions reproduced above, God is in a sense the object of motherhood: God is present in the world the way a child is enveloped within a womb, God is invoked as Angela's son, God is incarnated in Mary's womb as a still fetal yet already suffering Christ. These images hold a special interest for us readers if we note with Sara Maitland that "it is curious how little the image of God as child is allowed to surface,"[14] an unjust paucity that she appropriately relates to the fact that "child-care and children themselves have been given such a low status compared to the glorious work of abstracting and rationalizing."[15] But Angela also has recourse to those images of God as mother so dear to a certain medieval tradition.[16] Most openly, Angela compares God's embrace with that of a mother, the latter being implicitly posited as the epitome of a loving being: "Another way in which the soul knows that God is within it is by an embrace which God gives the soul. Never has a mother embraced her child with such love, nor can any person from this world be imagined who could give such a loving embrace" (62).

Although less direct, however, the most lasting images of the maternal aspects of God must come, in Angela's text as in that of other medieval mystics, from the representation of Jesus Christ. Aristotelian physiology, still prevalent during the Middle Ages, maintained that every child's flesh originated in the flesh of the mother (the father, on the other hand, provided the spirit). Since Christ had no human father, this connection with the maternal flesh was seen by many as being especially true of him: Christ's flesh was thus, in a sense, inherently and exclusively female. In his redemptive, sacrificial death through crucifixion, the flesh of Christ gave life to the world, just like a female body gives life by giving birth (which in the past was often a deadly process itself). This medieval perspective is recapitulated (though without any allusions to its medieval predecessor) in the contemporary feminist comparison of the Passion with the uniquely female birthing process – powerfully described by Sara Maitland in the following passage: "God also brought new life,

---

[14] Loades, 155.

[15] Loades, 155.

[16] These issues have been explored at length by Caroline Walker Bynum in her book *Jesus as Mother: Studies in the Spirituality of the High Middle Ages* (Berkeley: University of California Press, 1982).

gospel life to birth, stretched out for hours on the cross, autonomy removed by aggressive experts, the eternal Word reduced to wordless cries, bleeding down into the dark, overwhelmed by the sense of desolation, the doubt as to how much more you can put up with. And afterwards the joy, the new life, the sense of mystery and distance. It seems that the creative birthing of God as expressed in Christ's passion . . . can be given a deeper relating if we can learn to hear as holy the bodily experiences of women and trust the metaphor of God as mother."[17] This metaphor of the birthing God was very much alive in Angela's time and in Angela's work, since on the cross and in the Eucharist Christ gives us his body as food – just like women who breastfeed their babies give part of their own body as food (and we know that "the cult of the Virgin's milk was one of the most extensive in late medieval Europe," and that "medieval artists explicitly associated the lactating virgin with the Eucharist").[18] I will return shortly to an analysis of this set of images.

More generally, just as the body played a prominent role in the spirituality of medieval women mystics, it is also central to the concern of contemporary feminist theologians. In medieval theology, woman's association with the flesh was originally debasing: women could not accede to intellectual activity because their association with the body – through reproductive functions, first and foremost – made them incapable of using their minds to their full capacity. From an even more misogynous perspective, women had to be avoided as the ultimate carnal temptation, the primary source of sin. Yet many medieval holy women used precisely this association with the flesh in order to underscore their own proximity to Christ, thus deriving power from an ideology whose thrust was precisely to limit such power. A comparable situation can be perceived in theological reflections on the part of contemporary feminists. Women's association with bodiliness has far from disappeared, yet from such embodiment many women have derived eloquent authority rather than submissive silence. The "celebration of embodiment" has been described by Beverly Wildung Harrison as one of the basepoints for feminist moral theology: a feminist ethic must be for this theologian worldly and sensual, rooted in day-to-day activities and struggles, and it must never diminish the profoundly religious value of sustaining daily life (made up of activities traditionally carried out by women). The body is privileged in this worldview because our

[17] Loades, 154.
[18] Bynum, *Holy Fast*, 270–271.

ability to give, receive, and/or withhold love is rooted precisely in *"our bodies, ourselves*."[19] Indeed, according to Harrison, all our knowledge is ultimately mediated by our body insofar as it is rooted in our sensuality. This is perhaps one of the reasons why the symbolic production of women mystics has been so successful (one need only think of Margaret Mary Alacoque's "invention" of the devotion to the Sacred Heart of Jesus): it draws on the experiences of the body and of daily life, experiences readily understood by all.

For Angela of Foligno, spirituality is indeed rooted in sensuality, in "her body, her self." Bodily knowledge, for Angela, is not antithetical to and lower than rational knowledge, as medieval philosophers such as Thomas Aquinas would have it. Even that most debased and animalistic of all senses, the sense of smell, actively participates in her visions: "I often smelled indescribable odors" (45), she writes in the first supplementary step, and later she says that it is impossible to describe the "wonderful and indescribably delightful odor" that emanated from Christ's own mouth as she kissed him in the sepulcher (60). The senses of vision, hearing, touch, and taste, as can be seen in the excerpts quoted thus far, are essential to her mystical path, and they are related to Angela's insistent, continuous, almost obsessive focus on the body in its specificity. This is especially evident in the many descriptions of different body parts and their participation in visions and ecstasies.

Of course the body is not only the source of divinely-inspired pleasure. Pain and suffering are essential steps in the journey toward union with the divine. Although penance is not as prominent in Angela's *Memorial* as it is in many women mystics who were her contemporaries (and this is interpreted at times as proof of the scribe's intrusion in the composition of the *Memorial*), it is nevertheless clear that Angela's spirituality is shaped by its penitential aspect. The sixth supplementary step is where the most remarkable of these descriptions can be found. Not only do demons make her suffer, as Angela vividly recounts, like "someone hanging by the neck, with hands tied behind the back, eyes blindfolded, dangling from a rope – still alive, but without any help, without any support, without any remedy" (65). Angela causes her own suffering: "sometimes I become so angry that I can hardly keep from tearing myself to pieces; at other times, the anger is so intense, I can't stop beating myself horribly until my head and other parts of my body become swollen" (65). As horrible as this may sound today, medieval ascetic piety relied

---

[19] Loades, 204.

heavily on such practices. More specifically, in Angela's body "there is such a fire in the three shameful parts that I used to apply a hot flame to them, in order to extinguish that other fire, until you prohibited me from doing this" (66). The body can be exalted as a vehicle to ascend to God only if it is previously tamed of its impulses. These impulses do not correspond to all of sexuality, for it is clear that sexuality plays an important and positive role in Angela's itinerary: not a repressed sexuality, but one that leads to lasting rather than fleeting pleasure because it is linked with the experience of the divine. Rather, it is the unbridled sexuality which brings pain rather than pleasure, that must for Angela be extinguished. Only in this way – though through penitential methods with which we, like the scribe himself, can hardly sympathize – a harmony can be established between body and soul, between flesh and mind.

The celebration of embodiment, then, is connected to the desire and need to overcome the dichotomy between body and mind which in turn splits our intellectual and social lives – a painful split which Angela repeatedly heals. (Not coincidentally, this dualism has been linked by some thinkers to negative attitudes toward women.)[20] The very dichotomy between spirituality and social life, including politics and justice, needs to be dismantled: no better example can be adduced here than that of Saint Catherine of Siena, who derived from her spiritual experiences and divine visions the power to castigate prelates and even popes. Healing the personal as well as the social split, itself a painful process at times, takes place through both suffering and love. Angela's spiritual suffering frequently causes her to be physically ill: "whenever I saw the Passion of Christ depicted in art, I could not bear it; a fever would overtake me and I would become sick" (32), she says, and her confessor, more generally, states that "she was always very sick" (66). Even when it does not lead to pathology, the connection between the spiritual and the bodily is a real and perceptible one for this mystic: as Angela witnesses Christ's suffering, she says in the tenth step, "I was crying and weeping so feverishly that the tears began to burn my flesh; later, I had to cool my skin with water" (27).

From a positive viewpoint, Angela repeatedly notes the wholeness of her body and soul – mediated by language, mediated by God – such as when she makes the sign of the cross: "when I make the sign of the cross quickly and don't place my hand over my heart, I don't feel anything; but when I touch my forehead when I say, 'In the name

[20] Loades, 204.

of the Father,' and then touch my heart and say, 'and of the Son,' then immediately I feel a special love and consolation, and I seem to find the one I've named, there where I touch" (62). Through divine intervention Angela experiences a miraculous correspondence between words and things, signs and their referent, displaying a keen awareness of the functioning of language. Language, standing at the intersection of body and mind, becomes the mediator between physical and rational knowledge, as well as the vehicle to experiencing that which surpasses both body and mind.

Because her spiritual journey is also a physical one, Angela's mystical union with God is accompanied by a bodily union with Christ. In the fourth supplementary step, she claims: "At times it seems that my soul joyfully and delightedly enters into Christ's side" (57–58). She then describes a specific episode of this sort, during which "I collapsed to the floor and lay there speechless after this indescribable feeling of God began. . . . I lay there speechless, and without the use of my limbs. It was then that my soul seemed to enter Christ's side – and there was no sadness; in fact, my joy was so great that it can't be described" (58). The spirit of a woman enters the flesh of God, subverting the common sense that would instead characterize woman as flesh and God as spirit, and that would make their actual encounter unthinkable.

Yet paradox informs the mystical way. As Eleanor McLaughlin puts it, "God's lovers . . . demonstrated an ideal of Christian perfection which united contemplation and action, learning and piety, preserved individual gifts in the context of obedience to community, embraced common sinfulness in the joy of experienced forgiveness, and held together the realities of a God transcendent and immanent, all-might and all-love, father and mother. This mystery of contained paradox resisted even the deeply held opposites of body and soul, for that metaphysical dualism was tempered in a sacramental understanding of self and cosmos, microcosm and macrocosm."[21] Paradox is indeed the very essence of the mystic's journey: for McLaughlin, again, "sainthood or holiness was a pilgrimage towards God which supported a human nature of paradoxical and mysterious wholeness, paradoxical for us especially because it was an integration sought within the confines of celibacy."[22]

But the practice of celibacy in medieval piety must nevertheless be inscribed within the context of a spirituality in which sexuality

[21] Loades, 116.
[22] Loades, 116.

played an active part. If the spirit and the flesh seem antithetical to us, this was not the case for a mystic such as Angela of Foligno, from whom we may in fact learn ways of effecting a possible union between what we instead painfully perceive as unreconcilable opposites. This reconciliation, by the way, is also one of the objectives of contemporary feminist theology. Janet Morley, for example, claims that "our religious discourse is constructed *over against* the feminine," a negative term which carries associations, in addition to weakness, with sexuality and its chaotic emotions – "qualities that we as a culture, heavily valuing what have been seen as masculine characteristics, would much prefer not to know about."[23] But for Angela sexuality seamlessly fits within the spiritual journey she has undertaken. More specifically, Angela's sexuality, intended in its widest definition, is that of a middle-aged woman who has been married and has borne children, who knows what a male body looks like and feels like, who knows what bearing and delivering children means, who has nursed babies at her breast. She has experienced her body as pleasure-giving and pleasure-seeking, as capable of giving life through birth and of sustaining it through breastfeeding. All of this shapes her discourse, as the example of the nursing Christ will show in a moment. If her decision to shed all her possessions for Jesus has some illustrious precedents in the history of spirituality, none of them is as bold as her removal of her clothes to follow Christ as an attractive naked woman: "as I was standing near the cross, I stripped myself of all my clothes, and offered myself completely to Him. And although I was afraid, I promised to observe perpetual chastity and not to offend Him with any part of my body. I also accused every part of my body, one at a time, before Him" (26; Saint Francis's comparable stripping could not have been as scandalous, coming from a man and acquiring a political dimension by being performed in public).

Following the tradition of the *Brautmystik*, Angela repeatedly represents Christ's cross as her bed, and vividly describes the time she spent in Christ's sepulchre from the viewpoint of one who is very familiar with a man's body: "she first kissed Christ's chest, and saw that He lay there with His eyes closed, as He did in death; she next kissed His mouth from which she received a wonderful and indescribably delightful odor breathing forth from His mouth. Then there was a brief pause. Next she placed her cheek on Christ's and He placed His hand on her other cheek and held her tightly" (60).

23 Loades, 159–160.

Spiritual learning comes from the physical intensity of this erotic experience and not from its reduction to allegorical meaning. Nor can we claim such eroticism to be repressed: there is no indirectness, no lack of spiritual/physical satisfaction, no misunderstanding or misrecognition of the source and type of pleasure on Angela's part. Rather, the language used by this mystic is under her control, and she does not act like a puppet manipulated by the workings of a repressed or even just a sublimated desire.

Spiritual sexuality also emerges in the first supplementary step, when Angela returns several times to the beauty of Christ's throat and neck – itself read as bodily proof of Christ's divinity: "The beauty of His throat or neck was so great that I understood that it was due to His divinity; consequently, I seemed to see Christ's divinity through that beauty" (46). Significantly such beauty can only be compared, for Angela, to the beauty of the Eucharistic Host: both are flesh, and both have an aesthetic as well as a spiritual impact on the mystical lover. Christ's body is experienced both in pleasure and in pain, the two being intertwined with each other and with mystical spirituality. Toward the beginning of the *Memorial*, Angela describes a vision of Christ "showing all His wounds from His feet to His head. He even showed me the hairs of His beard, eyebrows, and head, which had been plucked out; and He counted every blow of the whip, pointing to each one" (27). Angela's attention to detail is striking, as well as necessary if her religious authority is to be based, like that of many holy women who were her contemporaries, on the visionary nature of her mystical experience alone. A similar impulse dictates Angela's focus – somewhat morbid, perhaps, in our eyes – on "those nails which I had heard pierced His hands and feet, and actually drove pieces of His flesh into the wood. And I desired to see at least that little bit of Christ's flesh which the nails had driven into the wood" (46).

The association between Christ's flesh as life-giving and the image of the nursing mother was a common one in the Middle Ages, as Caroline Walker Bynum among others has shown. Angela is not immune to this tradition, which she incorporates in her writings. I discussed above how her soul joyfully enters into the side of Jesus, thus penetrating his flesh. The bleeding wound at Christ's side is often represented in medieval art and literature as a breast that nourishes the hungry, who in turn feed from it. Sometimes Christ's own hand holds the flesh surrounding the bleeding wound the way a nursing mother holds her lactating breast. Angela herself uses this breastfeeding image when she writes: "He summoned me and told me to place my mouth at the wound in His side; and it seemed to me that I was seeing and drinking His blood as it was freshly flowing from His side" (29). Once more, spiritual life is intertwined with bodily processes for Angela: Christ's blood, signifying his salvific Passion, is the necessary nourishment for Angela's soul, and it can best be compared to the one food necessary for human survival, namely breast milk – the first, essential nourishment of every human being. This analogy must have been easier to understand for medieval people than it is for us in part because, according to medieval physiological theory, breast milk was nothing other than converted blood, so that a mother's blood quite literally becomes food for her children. But in general the equation of God with food is a prevalent one in the *Memorial*, where we read sentences such as "I began to have a taste of divine sweetness" (30), "I felt the first great consolation of God's sweetness" (32), "I am the Holy Spirit; I have come to give you a consolation, which you have never tasted before" (40), and numerous others along these lines.

The noteworthy association between Christ's body and that of a breastfeeding mother cannot be disentangled from the Eucharistic piety that was so prevalent among European holy women during the Middle Ages. From a "negative" perspective, this piety was tied to a fasting behavior reminiscent of what we now term anorexia nervosa (a gender-related disorder of the body).[24] Yet Angela, although she fasts for both spiritual and medical reasons ("she was always very sick and could only eat very little," 66–67), nevertheless "she was very plump and ruddy" (67). Food imagery pervades Angela of Foligno's writings and it takes multiple, spiritually interconnected forms: food is the motive for a daily activity to carry out for both self and others, especially the poor and the sick; food is a pleasure and a need to give up as penance through fasting; food is an image for the delights of God's word; and above all, food is Christ's body in the form of the Eucharist. Food is in Angela's writings both a quotidian and a miraculous entity. Preparing it and giving it to others sanctifies her daily existence, as when she is tempted by the devil while washing lettuce and when she sells her headveils to buy food for the sick at the hospital (56, 53). Giving up food by fasting allows Angela to control her unruly flesh, and allows her to imitate Christ, who says: "for you I suffered hunger and thirst" (41). Spiritual life comes even to replace food for Angela: "I experienced such delight in

---

[24] For more on this analogy, see Rudolph Bell, *Holy Anorexia* (Chicago: University of Chicago Press, 1985).

prayer that I forgot about eating. And I wanted not to need to eat, so I could remain in prayer" (32). Metaphors drawn from the realm of food then flow quite seamlessly from its daily material ubiquitousness into the spiritual realms of the miraculous: Angela says that she "began to have a taste of divine sweetness" (30), and that she "was told that an understanding of the Epistle was so delightful that anyone who understood it well would forget all worldly matters" (31). She repeatedly talks of God's sweetness: "I began to receive sweetness from God within my soul continually" (30), "I felt the first great consolation of God's sweetness" (32), "I felt an ineffable divine sweetness" (41). As Nicola Slee has noted while analyzing parables that speak especially to and of women's experiences, "The banquet image . . . speaks to women whose lives are very much bound up with the rituals of feeding and feasting."[25]

But the most profound experience of food that characterizes Angela's spirituality is her Eucharistic piety, which she clearly relates to the physical experience of eating in the following long passage from the fifth supplementary step, worth quoting at length: "when she receives communion, the Host lingers in her mouth; she said that it does not have the taste of bread or of any meat we know of. 'It most certainly has the taste of meat, but of a meat that has a most flavorful taste – I don't know what in this world to compare it to; it goes down sweetly in one piece, not in little pieces, as it used to.' She also mentioned how quickly the Host dissolves and does not remain firm as before. 'In fact, it is so sweet as it goes down in one piece that, if I had not been taught to swallow the Host quickly, I would gladly keep it in my mouth for a long time; but then I remember that I should swallow it quickly, and then that the Body of Christ immediately goes down together with that unknown taste of meat, and it goes down so completely that afterwards I don't have to drink any water. This is not what usually happens; usually, I have to make an effort to swallow the Host, so that there is none left between my teeth. But now it goes down immediately, and when it is down inside my body, it gives me an extremely pleasant sensation, which, as can be observed, causes me to tremble so violently, that I can drink from the chalice only with a great effort.' " (61). Like the proliferating Eucharistic miracles of medieval Europe, this passage of Angela's *Memorial* is firmly connected to the doctrine of transubstantiation and the piety out of which it developed: it was the Fourth Lateran Council (1215) which clearly defined the physical presence of

Christ's body and blood in the bread and wine consecrated at Mass. And so, in the thirteenth century the Eucharist became for the first time the object of adoration in addition to being, as it was from the time of the Last Supper, a communal meal that spiritually fed and united a group of Christians (thus, in 1264, the feast of the Corpus Christi was instituted). It should therefore not be surprising that for Angela the Eucharist tastes like the flesh into which consecration turns it.

Food is part of that world of creation praised by Saint Francis of Assisi and quietly present throughout Angela's work. This same creation is a focal point for the investigations of feminist theology. As Margaret Farley puts it, "Feminist theologians' concern for this theme [the meaning and value of the world of nature] is directly influenced by their concern for patterns of human relations and for the world as the place of human embodiment."[26] Similarly, Angela's spiritual journey takes place within the physical order of creation: this is exemplified by her descriptions of the vineyards through which she is journeying when the Holy Spirit speaks to her during her pilgrimage to Assisi (41). In Assisi, it is while Angela is looking at a stained-glass window depicting Saint Francis being embraced by Christ that God tells her she will also be embraced in the same way (43) – an obvious example of the interaction between public iconography and the mystic's private visions.[27] The love of God is described by Angela with the physical and quotidian image of a sickle: "she saw Love clearly coming towards her . . . immediately after it reached her, she seemed to see . . . that Love approached her like a sickle. . . . it moved like a sickle" (60). In spite of the mystic's protestations that by the movement of the sickle "one should not here understand a measurable or physical likeness" (60), still this physical love has physical effects, for "immediately following this experience she was filled with Love and boundless contentment which, although satisfying, nevertheless produced a very intense hunger – so extreme that all her limbs became disjointed" (60).

Like Christ's, God's love involves both Angela's spirit and her body as it strives to conform itself to the spirit and the body of its beloved. From this perspective, Angela's body is a malleable one,

---

26 Loades, 245.
27 This subject has been explored at length by Chiara Frugoni in "Female Mystics, Visions, and Iconography," in *Women and Religion in Medieval and Renaissance Italy*, ed. Daniel Bornstein and Roberto Rusconi, trans. Margery J. Schneider (Chicago: University of Chicago Press, 1996): 130–164.

prone to changes and dislocations as it attempts to model itself on Christ's. In Assisi, as Angela shouted for her beloved not to abandon her, she said that "all my joints were dislocated" (43). And when she feels Christ's love in her soul "all the parts of my body feel disjointed, and I want it to be like this; all the parts of my body feel the greatest delight, and I wish I could always be in that state. And my body parts make a noise when they are disjointed. And I feel this dislocation more when the Body of Christ is elevated, at which point my hands are disjointed and opened" (51)

The question of *imitatio Christi*, so central to the spirituality of Angela as well as to that of many of her contemporaries, can be related to the centrality of the Incarnation in contemporary feminist theology. As Rosemary Radford Ruether puts it, in an essay appropriately entitled "The Liberation of Christology from Patriarchy," "Today a Christology which elevates Jesus' maleness to ontologically necessary significance suggests that Jesus' humanity does not represent women at all. Incarnation solely into the male sex does not include women and so women are not redeemed. That is to say, if women cannot represent Christ, then Christ does not represent women."[28] This statement clearly alludes to the burning question of the ordination of women (our ability, that is, to represent Christ in the Church), but more generally and importantly Ruether doubts the extent to which women are able to identify with Jesus Christ as God Incarnate, given the imagery and language used to describe such Incarnation. For, as Ruether continues, "the emphasis on Jesus' maleness as essential to his ongoing representation not only is not compatible but is contradictory to the essence of his message as good news to the marginalized *qua* women."[29]

From this perspective, contemporary feminist theology has much to gain from an appreciation of the spirituality of women mystics such as Angela of Foligno, for whom Christ's flesh has uniquely female characteristics (although I also do not underestimate the submission of medieval holy women to a detrimental status quo, and their frequent allegiance to a misogynous ideology). We have already seen how the image of breastfeeding informs Angela's vision of herself drinking from Christ's wounded side, and how she is physically and spiritually nourished by divine food in the shape of the Eucharist. Through *imitatio Christi*, Angela identifies with Christ's flesh as it suffers and dies on the Cross – an identification aided by

[28] Loades, 140.
[29] Loades, 147.

the cultural gendering of Christ's flesh, in the Middle Ages, as female flesh. As Angela explains, "whenever I saw the Passion of Christ depicted in art, I could not bear it; a fever would overtake me and I would become sick. For this reason, my companion carefully hid all pictures of the Passion from me" (32). In Christ's suffering flesh, she saw and felt her own. Christ's pain on the cross is one with woman's pain here on earth. While Caroline Walker Bynum interprets this bond between women, food, flesh, and therefore Christ, as an empowering one that should free us from a distorted picture of medieval women as fleshly outcasts to the message of redemption, Grace Jantzen, on the other hand, sees this very identification of women with bodiliness, suffering, and salvation as part of a "world that feminists must find terrifying," because "the identification of women with the flesh, and with the suffering humanity of Christ, meant that the religious symbolism which went most deeply into the psyche was a symbolism which placed women to men in the role of the suffering servant."[30] Both points are strongly argued yet, as Bynum states at the end of her book, "Perhaps we should not turn our backs so resolutely as we have recently done either on the possibility that suffering can be fruitful or on food and female body as positive, complex, resonant symbols of love and generosity."[31]

In addition to the thorny question of the gender used to elaborate the conceptions of Christ, *imitatio Christi* can also be related to another concern of feminist theology, namely the role of the Crucifixion in our understanding of the Christian calling. In contrast with the exaltation of sacrifice for its own sake, Beverly Wildung Harrison notes that "Jesus' death on the cross, his sacrifice, was no abstract exercise in moral virtue. His death was the price he paid for refusing to abandon the radical activity of love – of expressing solidarity and reciprocity with the excluded ones in his community. Sacrifice, I submit, is not a central moral goal or virtue in the Christian life. Radical acts of love – expressing human solidarity and bringing mutual relationship to life – are the central virtues of the Christian moral life."[32] Angela's *imitatio Christi* underlines such an understanding of Jesus's death because it embeds love – for Christ, for the Other – in her experience of suffering: the divine Passion is also a human passion, for Christ's sacrificial death signifies a radical

---

30 Jantzen, 216, 223.
31 Bynum, *Holy Fast*, 301.
32 Loades, 210.

love for humanity that, like the Cross, is at the center of Angela's journey.

Thanks to the contrast between contemporary critiques of Christ's masculinization and the medieval gendering of Christ's flesh as female, Angela's reader can appreciate the theological and devotional relevance of the language used to describe the divinity – words as well as imagery. Feminists rightly complain that if Christ does not represent women as well as men, then how could women be included in the redemption he effected through his Incarnation? Ironically, on the other hand, medieval women saw themselves as being especially included in the redemption because of their association with the flesh and hence with Christ's own body – associations most visible to us in the prominent, though often overlooked linguistic traces they have left behind in their writings. In spite of a prevailing cultural misogyny, that is, images of Christ – linguistic as well as visual – were perceived as less androcentric in the Middle Ages than they are now because the use of gender imagery was more fluid, less literal.[33] Language is indeed a central concern for both feminist theologians and medieval mystics, especially Angela of Foligno. More generally, language is also a central topic of feminist theoretical discussions for obvious reasons: language has repeatedly excluded or devalued women's experiences both explicitly and through its hidden power to inform and create concepts and actions. The French feminist term *écriture féminine* and the controversies it has inspired provide a prolific instance of the conflictual relationship women entertain with language and especially writing (one critic even claims that "the mystic's discourse presents one of *the* most fully realized instances of *écriture féminine*").[34] Do women write differently? Is such difference, assuming it exists, perceptible to the reader? Is it a biologically-based difference contingent on the sex of the writer, or is it a way of writing that men as well as women are capable of practicing? And, ultimately, in what does such a difference consist?

The question of the imagery suitable in the descriptions of God, of the gender to be used when referring to God, the appropriateness of the word God itself, continue to be the subject of much feminist

---

33 On this subject, see Caroline Walker Bynum's essay "The Female Body and Religious Practice in the Later Middle Ages," in her book *Fragmentation and Redemption: Essays on Gender and the Human Body in Medieval Religion* (New York: Zone Books, 1991): 181–238.

34 Anna Antonopoulos "Writing the Mystic Body: Sexuality and Textuality in the *écriture féminine* of Saint Catherine of Genoa," *Hypatia* 6.3 (Fall 1991): 185–207, 202.

discussion. In spite of obvious disagreements between various currents and individuals, however, there is a consensus between feminists and non feminists alike about the inability of language to adequately express the divinity. It is precisely this consensus that mystics like Angela of Foligno repeatedly though subtly disrupt. As literary critic Paolo Valesio aptly puts it, the topos of ineffability is paradoxically "one of the richest for the development of linguistic structures in the West."[35] One way of suspending ineffability, for example, is through extreme versions of problematic rhetorical strategies such as oxymoron – Angela eloquently though paradoxically exclaims "for me to live is to die" (70). A word coincides with its opposite, speech with silence and, alternately, silence with speech. As the great scholar of mysticism Giovanni Pozzi claims, "the mystical experience, contrary to those who predicate it as the realm of silence and absence, is founded on the word around a presence: a word received and given."[36] For what would be the sense of mystical experience, the evidence of which is constituted by texts alone, if it were truly ineffable?

Nonetheless, the description of the divinity remains a contested site for feminists and non-feminists alike. This impasse underlines the central role language plays in any theological and, more generally, in any religious discussion. Feminist Christians regularly complain about the linguistic sexist inadequacies of their tradition. Rosemary Radford Ruether writes for example that, "although Christianity has never said that God was literally a male, it has assumed that God represents pre-eminently the qualities of rationality and sovereignty. Since men are presumed to have these qualities and women not to have them, the male metaphor has been seen as appropriate for God, while female metaphors have been regarded as inappropriate."[37] Gail Ramshaw notes that "interestingly, we speak of God as an animal or a natural phenomenon more easily than as a woman."[38] And Janet Morley asserts, more constructively, that "feminine terminology is currently very illuminating in the debate about how we may speak of God, precisely because it clearly draws attention to its own inadequacy . . . religious language cannot but be

---

35 Paolo Valesio, " 'O entenebrata luce ch'en me luce': La letteratura del silenzio," in *Del silenzio: Percorsi, suggestioni, interpretazioni,* ed. Giovannella Fusco Girard and Anna Maria Tango (Salerno: Ripostes, 1992): 15–44, 21. My translation.
36 Valesio, 29. My translation.
37 Loades, 138–139.
38 Loades, 170.

metaphorical in character; that is, pointing in an imaginative way to a reality that is, in the end, unsayable . . . it is no coincidence that the great mystics of the past . . . tend to combine a preference for silence, and a distrust of *any* particular conceptual formulations, with a writing style that is luminous with unusual and striking imagery – including the feminine."[39] Thanks to her awareness of the mystical tradition, Morley can insert a feminist concern for the description of God within the context of a more generalized linguistic inadequacy that can nevertheless be overcome – or at least temporarily bypassed – through the explosion of linguistic conventions.

This very awareness of linguistic inadequacy informs Angela of Foligno's writings, which abound in statements concerning the impossibility of describing God and the Word with human words: "Whatever I say about it seems to me to be blasphemous" (36); "It seems to me that I blaspheme. . . . to respond as I did seems to me blasphemous" (69); "everything I've just said speaks ill of and diminishes these things, so as to blaspheme against them" (73); "I can't speak of these gifts – since to do so would do more harm and blaspheme more than explain" (74); "My speaking about them damages them; that is why I say that I blaspheme" (75); "I may blaspheme in speaking or in mis-speaking about this (since I cannot accurately put it into words)" (75). Clearly the association between describing God and blaspheming is a powerful one, one that must be shocking to today's reader – especially because it appears in the writings of a holy woman officially declared "Blessed" by the Catholic Church. But it is also clear that Angela does not use the term in the sense we generally give to it today. What does Angela mean, then, when she claims that she blasphemes? How is what she says about God irreverent or even impious? One can only begin to answer this question, for it would certainly be paradoxical to even attempt to solve the issue of ineffability. From a devotional perspective, Angela blasphemes insofar as she oversteps the limits of approved doctrine and devotional schemes. Even in the different context of medieval mystical tradition, Angela's erotic images were rather extreme, at the very limit of orthodoxy. Linguistically, however, Angela's blasphemies are tied to her need to go beyond referential language and its inadequacy in representing the unrepresentable. Blaspheming is one way of circumventing the obstacle of ineffability – and in so doing it, blaspheming exposes ineffability, the impossibility of verbal articulation, as a paradoxical, self-destructive topos. By uttering and even dictating what she describes as blasphemies, Angela stretches and pulls language beyond its conventional limits – an action necessary if she is to describe her own experience of limits. (The fascination Angela holds for contemporary thinkers such as Luce Irigaray, Julia Kristeva, and especially Georges Bataille rests precisely on her focus on transgression and her experience of the limits.)

Linguistic transgression and the language of the holy go hand in hand for Angela of Foligno. This link becomes manifest in one notorious episode of the *Memorial*, with a reading of which I would like to conclude my essay. On Holy Thursday, Angela goes to a hospital to wash the feet of the lepers there, and then she drinks the putrid water used for the ablution (her gesture, however repugnant, was not an isolated one, since variations on this action were performed by other medieval holy women and men as well: Catherine of Siena, for example, drank pus and Catherine of Genoa ate lice). A leper's scab gets stuck in her throat, and Angela describes it as tasting as sweet as if she were taking Holy Communion. Many threads of Angela's experience converge in this important episode: her *imitatio Christi*, her Franciscanism, her Eucharistic piety, her transgressive devotion, her self-abjection, her direct (mystical) relationship with God. Like Christ (and Saint Francis) she communes with and serves the lowest segments of society, the outcast, which she identifies with the body of Christ and hence with the Eucharist – though she transgressively turns flesh into Host rather than Host into flesh. This experience is contingent on the overcoming of disgust, the embrace of abjection, the force of which allows Angela to entertain an unmediated relationship with the divinity – to the point of bypassing clerical mediation and unwittingly performing the act of consecration, forbidden to the laity and thus to all women.[40]

Yet Angela's disturbing action clearly goes beyond human solidarity. This is an abject activity, a violation of the proper order of things that is especially troubling because undecidably ambiguous, miraculous yet disgusting. It is an action that brings about a liberation from the limits imposed by disgust, by the social education of our senses. It allows the holy person to reach reality by shedding the appearances that make up propriety, what one might call the cultural order of the symbolic. The joy (*jouissance*) of unmediated contact with God, mystical union, is made possible by unrestricted discipline: Angela imitates Christ by washing a leper's feet on Maundy

---

[40] It should also be noted that in the second supplementary step Angela obtains absolution for herself and her companion, again without the mediation of a priest.

Thursday, just like Christ himself washed the feet of his disciples at the Last Supper – which Maundy Thursday celebrates (the choice of a leper reveals Angela's Franciscan affiliation by evoking the kiss Saint Francis gave to a leper). Angela accomplishes this *imitatio Christi* through an act of transgressive self-abjection that takes medieval Eucharistic piety to a loathsome extreme.

In order to overcome disgust, a strict discipline of self-denial is necessary, a discipline which also consists of an obedience to God that implies infraction of human social conventions – including the cultural value attached to the integrity of the body and the taboos of defilement. In imitating Christ, Angela also ingests him by sacramentally turning a bit of leprous, putrescent flesh into his crucified and resurrected body. This action falls within the purview of abjection because, by making the borders beween inside and outside pervious, it renders identity itself problematic. Language presumes identity and is therefore threatened by abjection. Language indeed shrinks from representations such as the episode of washing the leper's feet and drinking the putrid water, yet Angela forces language to comply beyond its abilities, beyond the laws of non-contradiction and into the realm of the paradoxical. Such linguistic usage, intrinsic to mystical discourse, must lapse into blasphemy, both in theological and in linguistic terms. Yet only in such blasphemy, in such transgression, can Angela discover the words she needs to narrate her otherwise ineffable experience of God.

Angela of Foligno's Contemporaries

Umiltà of Faenza (1226–1310)

L ike Angela of Foligno, Umiltà (whose birth name was Rosanese Negusanti) was married and had children, who died in infancy. After several years of marriage, she persuaded her husband to renounce married life and they both took religious vows at the Benedictine monastery of Saint Perpetua in the town of Faenza, located in Northern Italy. In 1254 Umiltà left the monastery to live in a cell, as a hermit, for twelve years. In this period she began composing her sermons and gathering a circle of disciples around her. After this experience of complete isolation, Umiltà founded a monastery near Faenza and then, fifteen years later, another one in Florence, where she spent the rest of her life and where she died in 1310. Like Angela of Foligno's, Umiltà of Faenza's life and writings are characterized by frequent transgressions of the behavior expected of women at that time: at first she refused to marry, despite her family's wishes; when she did marry, she prayed for something to happen to her husband, so that she could abandon married life and follow Christ; she miraculously acquired that literacy to which she would not have otherwise had access; she abandoned the convent in order to become a recluse; she authoritatively asserted her teaching role and wrote and delivered her doctrinal sermons in Latin – the exclusive language of the high culture of men, to which women normally had no access; finally, she repeatedly left the convent of which she was an abbess in order to build new communities.

Of Umiltà's written production, nine sermons remain. Composed in Latin prose, they contain prayers and meditations in which the author is very self-conscious of the need and urgency of communicating to others her own visionary experience (rather than a more general, impersonal theological interpretation) of the divinity. She and Angela of Foligno – though Umiltà's stature is not nearly so great – are the first Italian women who practiced a self-conscious doctrinal charisma. Umiltà's spirituality is characterized by a physicality that emphasizes the sense of touch and smell as well as sight, instruments that are considered to be essential to the elevation of her soul. Two themes emerge with special clarity from the *Sermons*: the dialogue with God the Father (unusual in the Christian tradition) and a love so intense that it borders on violence.

As is the case for Angela of Foligno, the body plays a fundamental role in Umiltà of Faenza's mystical understanding of God. The following excerpt, translated from her sixth *Sermon*, turns the traditional Christian symbol of the lamb into a double-gendered creature whose sexuality underlines two relationships: the connection between women and the flesh and the related link between human flesh and Christ. The lamb is Christ, whose sacrificial death takes away the sin of the world, and who is insatiably hungry for human repentance. Yet this divine hunger is one with the hunger of the little sheep, as the faithful soul – a female lamb, one whose maternal breasts desire to be filled with the milk of charity. Furthermore, this little sheep also wants to suck on the loving breasts of the Eucharistic lamb – an image reminiscent of the medieval religious and iconographical motif in which Christ as mother nourishes humanity through the blood flowing from the wound at his side, a wound clearly and significantly positioned where a nipple would be found (and this image of drinking from Christ's wounded side also appears, as we have seen, in Angela of Foligno's *Memorial*).

From the *Sixth Sermon*. In honor of Jesus Christ

O eternally exalted King, full of piety, humble and most sweet, supreme in charity, hear this little sheep, who bleats in hunger. O good shepherd of the flock, do not abandon me in this arid land, Lord. Lead me to a pasture where the grass is fresh, so that I may graze only on flowers and become fat, and so produce much milk. And then, Lord, give me the immaculate lamb, who gladly sucks on teets and is always hungry, so that he may always be satisfied by my teets, and never separate himself from them. Love divine, you know the lamb that I seek from you, and may that lamb be taken away from those who do not understand.

Let us explain and make clear who this hungry lamb is. You are the lamb of God, who has taken away sin by your blessed blood on the wood of the cross, and you, Lord, are always hungry for the remission of sins. You cannot be satiated. This little sheep, who bleats in hunger and seeks a pasture, where she can become fat, is the faithful soul wishing to remain with Christ, who is its pasture. And she wants to go to a new field, and pluck only flowers, and contemplate the beauty of her beloved, and with the desire of her heart wants to fill her teets with the milk of charity, and to enter the garden of her own true love, and to gather red and white roses, and to drink in the purity of the blood of the Passion from that white lamb who was lifted up on the cross for our sins. Moreover, this is his little sheep with the immaculate lamb, the faithful soul with Christ, who is her blessed love, who so desires that for which he is always hungry, and cannot be satisfied, because he finds only a little milk of love.

O King of eternal glory, I am asking you for holy alms: always allow me to carry out what you teach me. Show in me, through my actions, the words that I speak, for the praise of your name. Give yourself completely to me and do not hide yourself from me, if you, my most sweet Christ, are willing to console me. Make me, in all things, pregnant with love in all of my entrails and let me give birth to that love. I desire children who must produce fruit and who must always reproduce my inheritance in your honor. O sweet Jesus, joyful lover of lovers, glory of the angels, joy of the saints, come totally into my soul, do not delay, you who were conceived through love. And look at me with your eyes, you who see all that is hidden; nothing can be concealed from you. Think well, Lord, if you want to help me, and do not delay your coming any longer. You are my creator, who has fashioned me; you are my redeemer, who has redeemed me; you are my debtor, who has given himself for me on the cross out of love. I am a little sheep, who has become a pilgrim for your love; from the pasture you know what sort of grass I feed on, and you know whether my life is sweet or bitter. Do not be very surprised if I seek only love; consider the swords which pierce my heart and the blows and poison which lead me to death when I see the sinners' lot cast over them because of their actions. This is the law which you want to demonstrate: You are the Lord of all, you can decide that I am in the company of sinners. For this reason I ask you for sweet honey, your entire love, so complete, that I may not be deceived, and when the arrows of poisonous fire come, it may not be possible to condemn me. Lord, I want to report my works to you, because I am in falsehood, and you are in truth. Do not condemn me according to my sins; lavish me with you mercy.

O my sweetest Christ, I speak to you so that I may be taught what I seek from you. Therefore, the sorrow of my heart is not hidden from you; place your hand on it. You know well what sort of root has been planted, and how it has grown and propagated; it has taken my heart and mind, and has bound my soul with the chain of love. O Jesus, Son of the Virgin, sweet love, you have been the sower of virtues continually. May the root which has been placed in my heart not dry up; make it multiply.

This speech is expressed through similes, which are an impediment to those who do not understand. The root, which I mention, is the thinking of the heart, which grows with desire, and should perform the good through love. And if my root is planted, Lord, such that it pleases you, let its branches sprout, so that one may see clearly the leaves with flowers and fruit produced for the praise of your name. Furthermore, the root is always covered with soil, and cannot be discerned, except by the tree; but if the tree produces good fruit, the root can be considered true. Yet my root was struck by envy before the tree flowered and my enemies want to kill it.

O Jesus of Nazareth, highest in humility, give me holy alms tonight; on this your glorious birthday hear my prayers. Lord, you give rich gifts on your birthday: turn your merciful ear to my voice. By the love of the blessed Mother who carried you, and of her most holy womb where you came out of, and of her blessed breasts and the milk which you sucked, and of the blessed hands which swaddled you, o most holy one, give me this gift. And by the grace of that holy land where you were born, and of that worthy manger where you were placed, and of that most blessed hay on which you lay, do not despise my prayer. . . .

Margherita of Cortona (1247–1297)

What we know about the life of Margherita of Cortona, born in Laviano (near the shore of Lake Trasimeno, in central Italy), begins with a notable transgression: at sixteen, she ran away from her modest home with a rich young nobleman from Montepulciano, Arsenio, with whom she had a child. Margherita thus belongs to that group of late-medieval women who, like Angela of Foligno and Umiltà of Faenza, broke with the traditional image of holy women as cloistered virgins: their sanctity emerged instead in moments of rupture of the ordinary frameworks for female life – the family and the convent. At Arsenio's death nine years later, Margherita was an impoverished "illicit" widow (since Arsenio had never married her, she did not have the status of a widow) with a young son, and she was also rejected by her own family. This traumatic experience is at the basis of her conversion. She found support in the Franciscan convent in Cortona, where she made public penance, devoted her life to the service of the poor and sick, and entered the Franciscan Third Order (like Angela of Foligno) in 1275. In 1278 Margherita is credited with founding a confraternity and a hospital, which still functions in Cortona as the Ospedale di Santa Maria della Misericordia (whose special mission is the care of poor mothers and their children). In 1288 Margherita became a recluse near the church of Saint Basilio, cutting off all earthly ties with her son (who was seen as a living reminder of her sinful past) and intensifying her fiercely ascetic life of bodily mortification, prayer, meditation, and daily ecstasies while in dialogue with God. She died in 1297 at the age of fifty but was not canonized until the eighteenth century, after a radical transformation of religious thinking.

Margherita's story reaches us filtered through the Franciscan hagiographic voice of her longtime confessor, Brother Giunta Bevegnati, whose Latin *Vita* includes the transcription of Margherita's dialogues with Christ. Not surprisingly, Margherita often compares herself with Mary Magdalen. Her experience is characterized by a typically Franciscan convergence of a mystical dimension, separated from the world, and her active life of charity, immersed among the needy. Her language is marked like Angela of Foligno's by an insistence on the corporeality of the encounter with the divine, though Margherita is inexhaustibly bent on annihilating her physical beauty: her confessor must even forbid her from cutting off her nose. Her mysticism centers on love and the Cross, where she finds Christ as her father, her brother, and, finally, her bridegroom.

The excerpts that follow, translated from Brother Giunta Bevegnati's *Vita*, highlight Margherita's identification with the crucified, agonizing Christ and her consuming Eucharistic devotion – spiritual features which she shares with Angela of Foligno as well as with other contemporary holy women. The excerpts also point to that focus on Christ's feeding and nurturing female flesh (depicting his chest wound as a lactating breast) already encountered in both Angela of Foligno's *Memorial* and Umiltà of Faenza's *Sermons*.

From *The Legend of the Life and Miracles of the Blessed Margherita of Cortona* by Brother Giunta Bevegnati

From Chapter 5

After many days of tribulations had passed, Margherita received the body of Christ with great reverence and fear. When she did this, she heard Christ say to her in her soul: "Daughter, your charity is being attacked by gossips, but you will be crowned in heaven, for you will take pity on my blood, which was poured out on the cross, more than any creature alive today. Because although many weep over my most bitter death and the shedding of my blood, they do not weep as you do. Daughter, I experienced tribulations, and you will suffer tribulations, too; I labored, and you will also labor; I was the subject of ridicule, and your works will be ridiculed too; I am in glory, and you, by my mercy, will be raised up to it, too. But I tell you: your tribulations will increase."

Hearing the mention of tribulations, Margherita responded to Christ her spouse: "If my tribulations increase, your grace for me will also increase." And the Lord said to her: "You are beyond the first steps through which one comes to grace; but now, I want you to ascend to a higher state of knowing me." And Margherita responded: "Lord, if you are doing this for me, why leave me among such debilitating fears?" And the Lord said to her: "As I concealed and hid my power on the cross, so I hide myself from you for the growth of your crown; and so that you may know what you are like by yourself without me. There are many from the sect of my apostle Thomas, because they are late in believing the things taking place in you. Now, shout, 'Glory to God in the highest': this indicates a new change toward God the Highest. Shout, 'And on earth peace among people of good will' – meaning peace among populations of unfaithful Christians.'' . . .

On the feast of Saints Laurentino and Pergentino she said: "Lord, although I am not worthy to approach the sacrament of your most Holy Body, even so, I come to you as a a sick woman comes to a doctor and to medicine." Trembling, she received Christ's body and heard Him say to her: "I am the living bread, which has come down from heaven, and I am the lamb of God, who takes away the sins of the world. Do you want to come to my Father?" And she replied: "Lord, when I am with you, I am with the Father and the Holy Spirit." And the Lord said to her: "Do you believe this?" And Margherita answered, "Lord, you know all things; you know that I believe." At this the blessing was given and the Lord said: "Salute my mother, so that you will not doubt." And she said the Hail Mary up to, "Blessed is the fruit of your womb." And when she finished this salutation, the Lord said: "Daughter, do you love me?" And Margherita answered: "Lord, not only do I love you, but, if it would please you, I long also to be in your heart." And the Lord said: "Why do you want to enter my heart and not the wound in my side?" Margherita responded: "Lord Jesus Christ, if I am in your heart, I will be in the wound in your side, in all the places where the nails are, in the crown of thorns, in the gall and vinegar, and in the veil placed over your venerable eyes." And the Lord again asked, "Daughter, do you love me?" And Margherita responded: "No, Lord." Then the Lord asked her: "When will you love me?" Margherita replied:

"Lord, I will love you when I feel so sharply in my body some of the suffering which you endured for me, so that with my hands joined together, my soul will separate from my body." And the Lord said: "Wouldn't you want a different death?" And Margherita responded: "I do not desire a different death, because I should choose this death out of love for you and because of my faults." And the Lord said: "My wisdom is so great that I would know how to give you a sweet death in this pain." And Margherita responded: "Lord Jesus Christ, I would not want a sweet death; rather I desire to die in such bitter compassion for your sufferings."

Then for a third time the Lord questioned her saying, "Do you love me?" And Margherita responded: "Lord, if I loved you, I would serve you and I believe that no creature has ever loved you as much as you are worthy to be loved." And the Lord said to her: "You have spoken the truth." And giving glory to the Lord, she said: "I would want not only to love you, but, if it were possible, I would want to do more than to love you – so much do I desire your love. I am obliged to this as long as I consider my worthlessness, which surpasses that of all other creatures, and which is not worthy to reach the heights of your dignity, which has lowered itself so much for my wretchedness."

From Chapter 11

On the Friday of the second Sunday after Epiphany, after receiving reverently the Son of God, she said with great happiness in her spirit: "O ineffable joy of my soul! O priceless happiness, which I long for!" After saying this, she immediately turned to her angel and said: "By that care which you provide for me according to the mandate of the Eternal King, I pray you to show me a sign that I am in His grace!" For she was having quite a few doubts that the unspeakable fervors, which she was experiencing at the thought of her Maker and which often compelled her to tear her clothes to pieces, were a substitute for the intimacy of that divine voice. But the one who is consuming fire, from whom all holy fervor originates, spoke to her and said: "You are my sister, you are my daughter, you are a light placed in the midst of darkness, who will turn the night into day, you are a candle placed in the hands of sinners, and you will lead to me not only virgins, but also wives and widows.

And I say to you that you love me for your own consolation. For a perfectly ordered soul that loves me would not seek any consolation on earth; this is reserved for the soul in the blessedness of heaven. But you are like a child who desires to always remain at his mother's breasts, and immediately cries, sighs and screams as soon as he is separated from them even for a short time. . . . That is why I command you to come often to the wound at my side and suck there and taste what has flowed from it for the salvation of humanity."

Vanna of Orvieto (1264–1306)

Born near Orvieto in 1264, Vanna (a diminutive of Giovanna) was orphaned early in life – an unstable situation which, like widowhood for other women, put her at the margins of society at the same time as it freed her from family constraints and allowed her to follow Christ. She remained an embroiderer even after entering the Dominican Third Order. Although not a Franciscan, Vanna belongs like Angela of Foligno and Margherita of Cortona to the complex phenomenon of the thirteenth- and fourteenth-century flourishing of lay female sanctity, linked both to the mendicant orders (whose Third Orders underwent a massive growth), and to the changing social status of the artisan class, to which Vanna belonged. Her ecstatic experiences and prophetic gifts conferred upon Vanna the authority of spiritual advisor for the entire town of Orvieto. She died at the age of forty-two.

All we know of Vanna's life and mysticism is mediated by her Dominican hagiographer, Giacomo Scalza, who in his highly rhetorical *Legenda* recounts at length Vanna's bodily spirituality. Vanna of Orvieto's mysticism is in fact characterized by the prodigious ability of her body to conform itself to Christ's and the martyrs', so that when she hears of their death while in ecstasy, her body, as malleable as wax, takes the shape of each martyrdom – first and foremost, the rigidity of the Cross. But she also physically enjoys the pleasure of the Resurrection, and in fact spiritual pleasures made her fat (like Angela) in spite of her relentless abstinence from earthly foods.

The following excerpts from Giacomo Scalza's *Legenda* point to Vanna's extraordinary bodily phenomena (usually referred to as paramystical), and, more important, to her Eucharistic devotion – a prominent and characteristically female religious concern. Closely associated to the theme of fasting, the Eucharist is for Vanna as for many of her contemporaries the prime opportunity to approach, and even enter and become Christ's crucified humanity by eating his body and blood, physically present in the consecrated Host thanks to the miracle of transubstantiation. *Imitatio Christi* and Eucharistic devotion are thus inextricably intertwined: in both, the woman's body fuses with Christ's body so as to explore, through corporeal identification and interpenetration, the limits of his humanity. Both are examples of the incorporation of flesh into flesh, of the redemption of human and woman flesh through the Incarnation of God.

From the *Legend* by Giacomo Scalza

From Chapters 5–6: Holy bodies
She had fixed in her mind the Passion and the cross of Jesus Lord and Savior with such devotion that whenever she thought or heard something about it, she was completely dissolved in tears at the bitterness of her beloved. Indeed she continuously carried in her own body the mortification of the cross for her love of the Suffering One. On Good Friday, when Holy Mother Church, in order to move the piety of the faithful, annually reenacts Christ's Passion, which the Son of God endured out of pity for us, if one may say so, while drunken with love for our salvation – on that feast day, while she was meditating intensely on Christ's most cruel Passion, her spirit was absorbed in bitterness, she lost the natural use of her senses, her body stretched out in the shape of the cross, and remained rigid, pale, and insensible – just as the Lord's body had been fixed with scorn to the cross.

Those nearby, if anyone happened to be present at that time, could hear the violent cracking of bones, as her body was painfully extended; it was so violent that it seemed as though her limbs were being wrenched from their joints. One foot was placed on top of the other and the other body parts were stretched out and remain so immobile that each one could be cut or broken off, rather than moved. Furthermore, with her members extended in this way, she felt a very sharp pain and a debilitating sorrow; she remained this way, fixed on the cross with Christ, until the beginning of night. This happened to her every year on this day for the last ten years of her life; except for one time, since she was suffering excessively with fever, we believe that God spared her such great sorrows and pains.

Often on Holy Saturday and on the day of the Lord's Resurrection, while meditating on the glory of the Risen One, she was suddenly taken into such glorious rapture that no one doubted that she was being given a taste of the same glory as the Savior's. At those times her face seemed very bright and her eyes sparkled.

One time on the feast of the Assumption of Mary the most blessed mother of God, the reading told how she was assumed bodily into heaven. She was thinking of this with great jubilation in her heart, and little by little she began to be taken up into ecstasy and her body too began to be lifted off the ground. There she was in the air, her body elevated almost two feet, stretched out, with her hands reaching up to heaven, in the usual posture of one praying while prostrate. And so her spirit was elevated in such a way for a long time; and her body returned to the ground with the same lightness with which it had been lifted up into the air.

On the feast of the Saint Catherine the virgin, when her story was being told to her, it aroused in her joyfulness of heart and happiness of mind, and she burst out these words of devotion: "Rise up, most blessed Catherine!" After she said these words, immediately she forgot the heaviness of her body, and was lifted up into the air for some time.

While she was languishing with love for her Beloved, and drunk with holy fervor, with a certain anxiety of mind, she said: "O! How wonderful and unpleasant this is! – I cannot speak about my Beloved!" She said this, because, whenever she began to speak about Christ, or whenever she heard about Him, she immediately fell into an ecstasy of mind. Also in her daily meditation her soul was filled with such sweetness that afterward she cared very little for food for her body. Also she used to say, almost as a small consolation: "Is it not annoying for someone to eat an unpleasant food?"

From Chapter 6: A heavenly food made her full
One time, on the feast of the birth of the Lord, due to a bodily sickness she was suffering, she could not come to church and receive the body of Christ with all the others, as is customary for the faithful and especially those of her order. On the day after this feast an exceedingly wonderful heavenly light shone brightly above her. And as she was gazing at this attentively and delightedly, there appeared a very white Host proceeding from the light, which entered her mouth; and she immediately took it. And divine goodness, who is the true light – who declares, "I am the light of the world" – did not allow this virgin, chosen as a vessel of election and grace, to be deprived of the sacrament of the divine body on such a day (since she could not receive communion with the others).

I believe this other fact should not remain unsaid: although she ate and drank very little, she was so fat and stout and in good health that if one saw her without knowing who she was, that person would have thought that she made frequent use of baths and many other bodily delights. This would not be surprising, because she truly enjoyed an abundance of joy, though not of the body but rather of the soul, which came from frequently tasting heavenly sweetness. Thus (as she herself explained with simplicity) every day, while contemplating heavenly things, the sharpest part of her mind fixed itself upon God, whom she loved with all her heart, and she got fat in her soul with a sweet-tasting heavenly food, which filled her entire body all the way to its external lips.

Chiara of Montefalco (1268–1308)

What is best-known of Chiara of Montefalco's life is, significantly, the condition of her body after she died. The zealous nuns of her convent who performed an autopsy on her immediately after her death found, implanted in Chiara's heart, all the symbols of Christ's Passion: the crucifix, the crown of thorns, the three nails, the pillar, the whip, the lance, and the rod with the vinegar-soaked sponge. Furthermore, in her gall bladder they found what was interpreted as a symbol of the Trinity: three globes of equal weight and appearance, arranged in a triangle. Of course many were suspicious of these miraculous discoveries, including the man who was later to become Chiara's hagiographer. But the theologians, jurists and physicians who examined the findings ruled out the possibility of fabrication or artifice (naturally there were those who remained suspicious).

These discoveries, earthly signs of mystical union and sanctification, made sense to those who knew Chiara's spirituality, since her life as a recluse first and then as a cloistered Augustinian nun was characterized, in addition to harsh ascetic practices and visionary experiences, by an emphasis on Eucharistic devotion and on Christ's Passion, to which she mystically participated. This identification with the suffering, crucified God, namely with the highest expression of God's humanity, constitutes the apex of Chiara's affective mysticism, as well as its connection to Franciscan spirituality (Augustinians and Franciscans have each repeatedly claimed Chiara of Montefalco as a spiritual member of their order). In 1291 Chiara became abbess of her monastery, and her intense work and visionary activity – confirmed by the gifts of knowledge, prophecy, and miracle-working – made her a well-known figure as far as the papal court. She was greatly admired, for example, by that same Cardinal Giacomo Colonna who approved Angela of Foligno's text around 1296. Chiara died in her convent of Santa Croce in 1308, at the age of forty, but was not canonized until 1881 (similarly, it was not until the eighteenth century that Angela of Foligno was beatified and Margherita of Cortona canonized).

Unlike Angela of Foligno, Chiara of Montefalco has not left any writings, and we must rely on Béranger of Saint Affrique's biography (his *Life of Saint Chiara of the Cross*), where the physicality of Chiara's mystical relationship with God is repeatedly emphasized. Thus the emblems found in her heart at her death have the function of concretizing, of literally embodying her *imitatio Christi* in the course of the Passion. This is the most prominent theological theme in her spirituality. This emphasis was accompanied by severe bodily mortification as well as by a typically Franciscan and active dedication to others – the poor and the sick, especially the lepers.

In the following excerpt, we read of Chiara of Montefalco's devotion to Christ's Passion and of her active, painful identification with it. This *imitatio Christi* led to the physical incorporation, of which Chiara was quite self-conscious, of her spiritual experience into the bodily insignia discovered upon her death. The amazing tranformation of Chiara's body is read by the hagiographer as simply the reflection of her soul's ability to imitate Christ.

From *The Life of Saint Chiara of the Cross* by **Berengarius of Saint Affrique**

In a certain vision Chiara was holding in her hands in front of her chest a very beautiful lamb with the face of a boy; its wool was whiter than snow and softer than silk; it was delicate in every way. The lamb was looking at Chiara's face and she felt an unspeakable sweetness and love emanating from the lamb and from the lamb's eyes. Then this lamb went down into a deep pit, where a very tall stick was standing. The lamb, standing erect and almost supporting that stick, said, shouting: "You who sit at bountiful tables, look at the lamb who carried the cross." . . .

One time, a certain good-looking youth with a crown of flowers on his head appeared to Chiara. Taking the crown from his own head, he placed it on Chiara's as a sign of betrothal.

One day, while Chiara the virgin was burning with the desire mentioned above, God revealed and showed His Passion to her. At that moment of revelation she saw Christ who was nailed to the cross on a certain mountain, and she saw the Lord's mother at the foot of the cross weeping and a great crowd of people standing around and causing an uproar, and she saw other events of the Lord's Passion, such that the whole manner and sequence of His Passion was revealed and shown to her by the Lord. In fact, as God told her, she saw everything that happened at Christ's Passion; everything was shown to her, as if she stood in person at the foot of the Lord's cross on the day of His crucifixion. This vision returned to her so often that she united herself to the Passion of Christ with so much compassion that she often felt inexplicable pain in her body. She could taste no flavor at all in food or drink. Everything to her was tasteless and bitter, as if she had swallowed the drink Christ had received on the cross.

She was experiencing very strong raptures, sometimes once a day, sometimes more, and sometimes one rapture alone lasted for many days. In these raptures Chiara's face was at times red, at other times pale, and sometimes during the same rapture her face changed color many times. Sometimes her entire body moved swiftly, sometimes it was completely still. Her body at times stood erect, like a statue, or else she was sitting, or kneeling, or lying down. These raptures were so strong and so frequent (and they lasted from Chiara's adolescence until her death) that they weakened her very much, and her companions at the monastery were constantly worried and afraid that Chiara would die during these elevations. After her raptures she remained very weak, and during her raptures she lost the power of her bodily senses.

Although nothing could be known with certainty about the visions and revelations which Chiara was having during these raptures, not even what she herself related with great difficulty and in an incomplete and obscure manner, even so, signs of her holiness can be well grasped from some words which she sometimes uttered during these raptures (although, for the most part, she was not in control of herself). Once during these elevations, although she was lying sick, her body, which she had been unable to move for a long time, began to move very quickly. And when she was in this condition for a while, she spoke and said: "Let me go, let me go!" Then she said: "Take me with you!" Then she lifted up her arms, raised herself to a sitting position, while her companions watched in amazement, because for a long time she had been immobile and unable to move. And she said: "Everything is burning, everything is burning, and you, what are all of you doing?" Later she began to sing sweetly and say: "How do the saints serve you, my love? They serve you with songs. Let me play that instrument again, my love; let me see my soul enter into yours." Then she said clearly and lovingly: "I was truly a fool, because I was afraid, but I had no reason to be afraid." And she kept repeating these words. Then she called on the Blessed Mary and the saints and spoke to them as if they were present; among others, she invoked Saint Francis saying: "Saint Francis, pray for me." One day, then, the sisters who had heard those words were telling this to another sister who had not been there that time. They were doing this in a place far away from Chiara, so that she could not possibly hear them with her bodily ears. However, Chiara then summoned another sister and said to her: "What are they saying and why? Do they believe that these things come from my spirit? My conscience tells me that I am the worst woman in the world; I don't see anyone worse than I am." What Chiara saw in that elevation is not known, but a certain holy woman, who had once been a nun in that same monastery, reported that Chiara at that time was made certain of her own salvation.

Many very trustworthy people, who knew Chiara well, believe that at various times she saw Christ perform every action which He had done in His life on earth. . . .

A very beautiful youth, the Lord Jesus Christ, appeared to Chiara while she was praying; He was dressed in white clothes, and carried a cross on his shoulder, equal in size and shape to the true cross on which he was crucified. He said to her: "I am looking for a strong place where I can plant this cross. Here I have found a suitable place to plant my cross." And Christ also added: "If you want to be my daughter, you should die on the cross." After this vision and revelation, Chiara said that she believed that God was performing great deeds in that monastery.

Because of this it is believed that the virgin Chiara, given the name 'of the cross,' from that time on possessed in the heart of her body the cross and all the signs of Christ's Passion – not just images, but tangible, physical signs. And one arm of the cross which she carried in her heart pierced through her heart itself, perforating it all the way to its exterior. This was known to all who wanted to see it after Chiara's death. Chiara herself during the sickness which sent her out of this world said five times that she possessed the Cross of Christ in her heart.

Annotated Bibliography

I have gathered here the books and articles on Angela that I have found especially useful in my research and that I think will be of use to those who want to approach Angela more closely. Some of these texts may not deal explicitly with Angela of Foligno but nevertheless discuss issues that are central to this author. This is a selection, for the bibliography on Angela is of course much wider; for more specific essays on Angela one should turn to the extensive bibliography provided by Ludger Thier and Abele Calufetti in their 1985 edition of Angela's writings. The texts are in English unless noted otherwise.

Primary texts

Angela of Foligno. *Complete Works.* **Translated with an introduction by Paul Lachance, O.F.M. Preface by Romana Guarnieri. New York: Paulist Press, 1993.**
This is a must for anyone who wishes to read in English the complete text of Angela's *Memorial* and the *Instructions* associated with her. The introduction is very useful, providing an extensive overview of Angela's life and times, information concerning the composition of her book, and a detailed discussion of Angela's spirituality – as well as of her influence on both her contemporaries and the following centuries.

———. *Il libro della beata Angela da Foligno.* **Edizione critica. Ed. Ludger Thier, O.F.M., and Abele Calufetti, O.F.M. Grottaferrata: Editiones Collegii S. Bonaventurae ad Claras Aquas, 1985.**
So far this is the definitive edition of Angela's *Liber*, based on seventeen Latin manuscripts. This book includes a valuable and detailed introduction, an extensive bibliography, and a medieval vernacular Italian version on the pages facing the Latin text. In Latin and Italian.

———. *Il libro dell'esperienza.* **Ed. Giovanni Pozzi. Milan: Adelphi, 1992.**
An anthology, translated into Italian, of Angela's *Liber* by one of the foremost contemporary scholars of mysticism, this edition, unlike most others, addresses itself to a general reading public (rather than to an academic or pious one). It includes a challenging general introduction (which analyzes Angela's work, context, and legacy more perceptively and in depth than any other introduction), more specific brief

contextualizing introductions to each cluster of anthologized excerpts, a bibliographic essay, and, at the very end, a useful paraphrased summary of Angela's *Memorial*. In Italian.

Secondary texts

Arcangeli, Tiziana. "Re-reading a Mis-known and Mis-read Mystic: Angela da Foligno." *Annali d'italianistica* **13 (1995): 41–78.**
Written from a loosely feminist perspective, this eclectic study examines Angela's *Memorial* both in terms of textual tradition (the issues of editions and of a male scribe's intervention) and in terms of its narrative development as an instance of Julia Kristeva's "women's time" and Hélène Cixous's "*écriture féminine.*"

Beckwith, Sarah. "A Very Material Mysticism: The Medieval Mysticism of Margery Kempe." In *Gender and Text in the Later Middle Ages*. Ed. Jane Chance. Gainesville: University of Florida Press, 1996. 195–215.
Drawing on both Lacanian psychoanalysis and the feminist philosophy of Luce Irigaray, this essay examines the potential of women's mysticism to undermine the claim to God's unrepresentability and neutral transcendence. At the same time the author remains critical of the effectiveness of the victimization and passivity of those holy women who conformed their body to Christ's Passion in order to gain access to words and the Word.

Bell, Rudolph. *Holy Anorexia.* **Chicago: University of Chicago Press, 1985.**
This psychological study of Italian holy women's fasting behavior (1200 to the present) in light of the modern anorexia diagnosis includes a detailed analysis of Angela of Foligno's story. In Bell's view, Angela is extraordinarily articulate in explaining the motivations that impelled some married women to holy anorexia: the war against the body, manifested in ascetic masochism, represented for them part of a struggle for liberation from a patriarchal family and society.

Bynum, Caroline Walker. *Holy Feast and Holy Fast: The Religious Significance of Food to Medieval Women.* **Berkeley: University of California Press, 1987.**
Although neither limited to Angela of Foligno nor even to Italy, this interpretive study in social and religious history is indispensable for understanding the role of food as symbol for Angela and her thirteenth- and fourteenth-century contemporaries. For these women, according to

Bynum, food – a basic symbol derived from ordinary female experience – was a way of controlling both self and environment. But just as important, even as ordinary food was renounced, Christ as food allowed holy women to become the crucified body that is the Eucharist – the suffering and feeding humanity of Christ.

Coppini, Beatrice. *La scrittura e il percorso mistico. Il Liber di Angela da Foligno*. Introduction by Adelia Noferi. Rome: Ianua, 1986.
A close reading of several passage of Angela's *Liber*, this book is written from a perspective influenced by much contemporary linguistic theory. Of particular interest is Noferi's theoretically sophisticated introduction, an original reflection on the status of mystical discourse within linguistic and semiotic theory: mysticism is here described as a transgressive discourse that mediates between two otherwise incommunicable spaces – the human and the divine, body and spirit, knowable and unknowable. In Italian.

De Certeau, Michel. "Mystique." *Encyclopaedia Universalis France*. 20 volumes. Paris: Encyclopaedia Universalis France, 1968. Volume 11, pp. 521–526.
A thorough introduction to the concepts and issues of mysticism by one of the greatest scholars of mysticism of all times, this brief essay is divided into three parts: the modern status of mysticism (including its etymology and its relation to geography, history, and psychologization), mystical experience proper (its paradoxes, its languages, and the link of the spirit with the body), and the role played by mysticism in different world religions. In French.

Finke, Laurie. "Mystical Bodies and the Dialogics of Vision." In *Maps of Flesh and Light: The Religious Experience of Medieval Women Mystics*. Ed. Ulrike Wiethaus. Syracuse, NY: Syracuse University Press, 1993. 28–44.
Although not primarily concerned with the work of Angela of Foligno, this is a brilliant and influential essay that argues for the interpretation of mysticism as a set of cultural and ideological constructs (as opposed to its traditional view as a manifestation of an individual's internal affective states). Communal and dialogic rather than private and passive, the discourse of medieval women mystics (of whom Angela is for Finke a prime example) succeeds in acquiring secular and spiritual empowerment and self-determination through verbalized visions as well as, ironically, bodily self-torture.

Irigaray, Luce. "La mystérique." In *Speculum of the Other Woman*. Trans. Gillian C. Gill. Ithaca: Cornell University Press, 1985.

In this dense and challenging chapter, the noted feminist psychoanalyst makes powerful and attractive claims for mysticism, which she posits as a source of dissent from and dissolution of the patriarchal social and symbolic order. These traits link mystical discourse with the female gender and place both outside of the male system of representation. Instead, Irigaray contends, female mysticism celebrates women's access to the imaginary and to *jouissance*.

Jantzen, Grace. "Feminists, Philosophers, and Mystics." *Hypatia* 9.4 (Fall 1994): 186–206.

Through a persuasive feminist argument against the link between ineffability and the mystical way, this article claims that the relegation of women mystics to the private, subjective, and inexpressible sphere has unjustly stripped their spirituality of its socio-political relevance and authority.

———. *Power, Gender, and Christian Mysticism*. Cambridge: Cambridge University Press, 1995.

This book includes the above article as well as other powerfully argued chapters that discuss the historically changing understanding of who counts as a mystic. This process of inclusion and exclusion, central to the formation of the mystical canon, is seen by the author as a shifting, gender-related social construction: the mystic is defined not only on the basis of that individual's experiences and beliefs, but also, and more important, on the basis of issues of power and gender. Thus, for instance, fourteenth-century Italian women could be counted holy only if they conformed to the identification of women with the flesh and with the suffering humanity of Christ.

Lachance, Paul, O.F.M. *The Spiritual Journey of the Blessed Angela of Foligno According to the Memorial of Frater A*. Rome: Pontificium Athenaeum Antonianum, 1984.

This thesis by the leading American scholar on Angela of Foligno contains a very useful introduction to and discussion of her life, times, and spirituality, and it develops a special emphasis on the issues related to Angela's inner journey: the patristic and theological tradition that preceded Angela and the purification and elevation that form the last supplementary steps of the *Memorial*.

Lavalva, Rosamaria. "The Language of Vision in Angela da Foligno's *Liber de vere fidelium experientiae.*" *Stanford Italian Review* 11.1–2 (1992): 103–122.
The essay examines Angela's sensorial acquisition of knowledge and the concreteness and immediacy of her expressions and images. Both body and spirit are thus included in the cognitive process that makes up Angela's mysticism: vision and eroticism are transformed in her writings into a noetic experience.

Leonardi, Claudio. "Portrait d'une mystique italienne du XIIIe siècle: Angèle de Foligno." In *La femme au moyen âge*. Ed. Michel Rouch et Jean Heuclin. Mauberge: Ville de Mauberge, 1990. 69–74.
Written in French, this brief essay is a very good introduction to Angela's life and spirituality. It explores important issues in Angela's *Liber* such as blasphemy, nothingness and annihilation in God, and Angela's relationship with the spirituality of Saint Francis. Leonardi identifies three steps in Angela's mystical path: love, nothingness, and resurrection. In French.

Leonardi, Claudio, and Enrico Menestò, eds. *S. Chiara da Montefalco e il suo tempo*. Firenze: La Nuova Italia, 1985.
Central for any study of Saint Chiara of Montefalco, this collection of essays also contains more general discussions of medieval female sanctity. Of particular interest is Silvestro Nessi's contribution on the spiritual relationship between Angela of Foligno, Chiara of Montefalco, and Jacopone da Todi, and Chiara Frugoni's discussion of the intense connection between iconography and the visions of women mystics. In Italian.

Lochrie, Karma. *Margery Kempe and Translations of the Flesh*. Philadelphia: University of Pennsylvania Press, 1991.
This book is very valuable for scholarship on Angela of Foligno because, in addition to a perceptive examination of her mysticism, it also contains original and helpful discussions, from a feminist cultural-historical perspective, of the relationship between women, the body (particularly the issue of *imitatio Christi*), and the mystical undertaking (including an analysis of the controversial case of Chiara of Montefalco).

Mazzoni, Cristina. "Mysticism, Abjection, Transgression: Angela of Foligno and the Twentieth Century." *Mystics Quarterly* 17 (June 1991): 61–70.
The essay analyzes the relevance of Angela of Foligno in the writings of three twentieth-century French thinkers: Simone de Beauvoir, who in

The Second Sex uses Angela as an example of the erotomaniac nature of mysticism and its relegation of women to patriarchal subjection; Julia Kristeva, in whose *Powers of Horror* Angela appears as an instance of the link between self-abjection, Christian mysticism, and the sublime; and Georges Bataille, in whose *Guilty* Angela is the model to be followed in order to attain mystical ecstasy even in the absence of God.

————. "On the (Un)representability of Woman's Pleasure: Angela of Foligno and Jacques Lacan." In *Gender and Text in the Later Middle Ages*. Ed. by Jane Chance. Gainesville: University of Florida Press, 1996. 239–262.
The subject of this essay is the controversy regarding the possibility of linguistically representing the female body, and particularly its pleasure. While the well-known thesis of French psychoanalyst Jacques Lacan, in *Encore*, is that woman cannot be put into words because she is not "whole" with respect to language – and thus, like mystical experience (which he sees as peculiarly feminine), her pleasure or *jouissance* is for Lacan ineffable – Angela of Foligno's *Memorial*, in spite of its protestations concerning the difficulty of expressing with words the encounter with God, repeatedly and successfully articulates the pleasure, both spiritual and bodily, experienced in the course of her mystical path.

————. *Saint Hysteria: Neurosis, Mysticism, and Gender in European Culture*. Ithaca, NY: Cornell University Press, 1996.
This book examines the interpretation of women's mysticism as an expression of the quintessential female malady, hysteria. It analyzes several different types of texts – religious, medical, psychoanalytical, literary – in order to trace some of the ways in which the identification of mysticism with hysteria became prevalent. The fourth chapter deals most closely with the discourse of women's mysticism, particularly with the works of Angela of Foligno and the turn-of-the-century Italian Saint Gemma Galgani.

Mooney, Catherine M. "The Authorial Role of Brother A. in the Composition of Angela of Foligno's *Revelations*." In *Creative Women in Medieval and Early Modern Italy: A Religious and Artistic Renaissance*. Ed. E. Ann Matter and John Coakley. Philadelphia: University of Pennsylvania Press, 1994. 34–63.
Against previous scholars' claims concerning Angela's sole authorship of the *Memorial* and her scribe's unobtrusive mediation and translation, this essay argues (supported by abundant textual evidence) for Brother A.'s active intervention in and shaping of Angela's book, thus

establishing his role as an energetic collaborator rather than an insignificant accessory.

Movimento religioso femminile e francescanesimo nel secolo XIII.
**Atti del VII Convegno Internazionale, Assisi, 11–13 ottobre 1979.
Assisi: Società Editrice di Studi Francescani, 1980.**
A very useful collection that discusses the historical and spiritual background for Angela of Foligno's experience, with essays dealing with, among other issues, female monasticism, the experience of Chiara of Assisi, and, of course, the relationship between Saint Francis's message and legacy and medieval women. The book includes an excellent essay by André Vauchez on the changes that the ideal of female sanctity underwent during Angela's time, the thirteenth and fourteenth centuries. Primarily in Italian with one essay in French and one in German.

Petrocchi, Giorgio. "Astrattezza e realismo nel *Liber* della beata Angela da Foligno." *Lettere italiane* **8 (1956): 311–318.**
Through a stylistic analysis of Angela's poetics, literary critic Petrocchi identifies in her *Liber* both an ecstatic (abstract and antirealistic) and an ascetic (concrete and material) tone, converging in a speculative mysticism which ultimately aims to dehumanize the mystical experience by detaching it from all that is human. In Italian.

Petroff, Elizabeth Alvilda. "Writing the Body: Male and Female in the Writings of Marguerite d'Oingt, Angela of Foligno, and Umiltà of Faenza." In *Body and Soul: Essays on Medieval Women and Mysticism*. New York: Oxford University Press, 1994. 204–224.
This analysis of the effects of gendered corporeality on the writings of three medieval women mystics shows how bodily imagery, combined with a peculiar use of syntax (Petroff invokes, though at a superficial level, the French feminist notions of *écriture féminine* and *jouissance*) can be used to subvert rather than reinforce gender stereotypes.

Pozzi, Giovanni, and Claudio Leonardi, eds. *Scrittrici mistiche italiane*. Genova: Marietti, 1988.
This important anthology of Italian women mystics from the 1100s to the 1970s contains excellent, concise introductions (biographical as well as spiritual) to each writer, including, of course, Angela of Foligno, two brilliant introductory essays (one on women's mysticism and the other on women's sanctity), extensive bibliographies on each writer, a very useful bibliographical essay on various aspects of mysticism, and a brief yet profound dictionary of mystical terms. In Italian.

Sagnella, Mary Ann. "Carnal Metaphors and Mystical Discourse in Angela da Foligno's *Liber*." *Annali d'Italianistica* **13 (1995): 79–90.**
By examining Angela's perception of the female body in relation to the predominantly negative notions of womanhood in the Middle Ages, this study posits her self-defilement and self-abjection as essential to Angela's spiritual undertaking. It is only with the bodily dissolution brought about by mortification and asceticism that the body-soul duality dissolves and mystical union with Christ can be attained.

Sante e beate umbre tra il XIII e il XIV secolo. Chiara d'Assisi, Agnese d'Assisi, Margherita da Cortona, Angela da Foligno, Chiara da Montefalco, Margherita da Città di Castello. Mostra Iconografica. **Foligno: Edizioni dell'Arquata, 1986.**
In addition to a series of essays on the medieval Umbrian holy women who appear in the title, the book includes a fascinating collection of reproductions of these women's iconography. Each of these pictures is introduced by a short text that puts it into its spiritual and historical context and explains the relevant iconographical choices made by the artist. In Italian.

Schmitt, P. Clément, O.F.M., ed. *Vita e spiritualità della beata Angela da Foligno.* **Perugia: Serafica Provincia di San Francesco ofm Conv., 1987.**
A wide-ranging collection of essays, mostly written in Italian, this book covers numerous aspects of contemporary scholarship on Angela: her spiritual theology, the historical, geographical, and spiritual contexts of her experience, the popularity of the *Liber* through the centuries, her relationship with Saint Francis, Ubertino of Casale, and Christ, her Eucharistic piety, her approach to poverty, her iconography, and an overview of her cult in Italy and abroad. The essays are written from a traditional Catholic perspective, and the book significantly bears the *imprimatur* of a Franciscan delegate. Primarily in Italian with one essay in French, one in English, and one in German.

Slade, Carole. "Alterity in Union: The Mystical Experience of Angela of Foligno and Margery Kempe." *Religion and Literature* **23.3 (1991): 109–126.**
This well-argued essay analyzes the mysticism of Angela of Foligno and the English mystic Margery Kempe (c.1373–c.1440) through a comparison with Luce Irigaray's psychoanalytic version of women's mysticism and the female aspect of the divine in "La mystérique" (in her book *Speculum of the Other Woman*). Unlike Irigaray, the two medieval

mystics experience God as radically other, and it is to this very alterity (and to their union with it) that they owe their empowerment as subjects in the world.

Index

CPSIA information can be obtained
at www.ICGtesting.com
Printed in the USA
BVHW03s1229060818
523431BV00030B/88/P